THE IMPOSSIBLE CLIMB

THE
IMPOSSIBLE
CLIMB

Alex Honnold, El Capitan, and a Climber's Life

By Mark Synnott

Adapted for Young Readers by Hampton Synnott

VIKING

VIKING
An imprint of Penguin Random House LLC, New York

First published in the United States of America by Viking,
an imprint of Penguin Random House LLC, 2021

This work is based on *The Impossible Climb: Alex Honnold, El Capitan, and the Climbing Life*, by Mark Synnott, copyright © 2018 by Mark Synnott, published by Dutton, an imprint of Penguin Random House LLC.

Visit us online at penguinrandomhouse.com.

LIBRARY OF CONGRESS CATALOGING-IN-PUBLICATION DATA IS AVAILABLE.

Printed in the United States of America

ISBN 9780593203927

10 9 8 7 6 5 4 3 2 1

Design by Lucia Baez
Text set in Metro Nova Pro

This is a work of nonfiction. Some names and identifying details have been changed.

The publisher urges anyone who would take up rock climbing to take all proper precautions, seek out training from experienced climbers, use protective gear, and practice on easy climbs before moving on to more challenging climbs.

For Tommy, Lilla, Matt, and Will

"El Cap is only a matter of time, but that time is looking shorter all the time. I remember when the idea of even a free El Cap route was almost inconceivable but somebody soloing it? We have to be very careful about what we believe to be impossible."   —KARL BRALICH,

SuperTopo climbing forum in 2008

INTRODUCTION

The chapters of this book come together to create a riveting story about pushing the limits of human potential. Alex Honnold achieved what many deemed utterly impossible, and my husband, Mark, was there to witness the making of greatness every step of the way.

But if we focus solely on how this story ends, it's easy to misunderstand Alex's motivations when we hear about him climbing a cliff three times higher than the Eiffel Tower without a rope. And we overlook the process that got him there. What I learned from immersing myself in this story is that climbers like Alex and Mark are no different from acrobats, race car drivers, surgeons, or anyone else who spends years honing their skills. But I find that we react differently when we see acrobats flying from trapezes or race car drivers zooming around the track. We give them credit for the years of training and practice it took to master their craft. We don't assume we can walk out on a tightrope without the same preparation. And so I urge those who open this book to do the same here. At the heart of this story is the fact that Alex only sets off on his historic ascent after completing a nine-year program of physical and mental training, which he undertook even though he never really knew if his dream was actually attainable.

As a kid I enjoyed sports like skiing, lacrosse, soccer, and sailing. I knew about rock climbing, but something about it seemed a little too far out there, and I assumed that climbers were gifted with physical and mental "superpowers" that I would never possess. Years later, though, as climbing gained popularity, I began to dabble a bit with the sport, first on small rocks in the woods, but eventually on taller cliffs.

As I grew older, I began to meet more and more climbers, and over time, I realized that maybe they weren't as different from me as I thought. Maybe anyone can climb. Maybe climbing is in our DNA. These days, rock climbing has gone mainstream, and many people have at least tried the sport on an indoor wall. Climbing is now one of my favorite family activities, and I can't think of anything that is more empowering for our children, who range in age from four to twenty-one, than a day spent bonding and testing their limits at the cliff. It's because of this that I jumped at the opportunity when Mark asked me if I might be interested in adapting *The Impossible Climb* for young readers like you.

I want all children reading this story to know that as long as they're willing to invest the time and energy required to achieve their dreams, it's okay to take risks. Because without people who are willing to explore the boundaries of human potential, the world would be a far less interesting place to live. Perhaps it was Helen Keller who put it best when she said, "Avoiding danger is no safer in the long run than outright exposure. Life is either a daring adventure, or nothing." I'm sure Mark and Alex would agree. What do you think?

PART ONE

YOUTH

CHAPTER ONE
The Hon Is Going to Solo El Cap

Jimmy Chin took a deep breath, puffed out his cheeks, and exhaled slowly. "There's something I need to tell you," he whispered. "Can you keep a secret?"

We were in the giant red tram, traveling four thousand feet to the summit of the Jackson Hole Mountain Resort, standing chest to chest and surrounded by a hundred other ruddy-faced skiers all looking forward to a long powdery run from the summit. Jackson Hole, located in western Wyoming next to the Grand Teton National Park, is famous for its difficult terrain, deep powder, and the many world-class big-mountain skiers who call it home. The highest peak in the range, the Grand Teton, tops out at 13,775 feet and welcomes thousands of climbers annually. Climbing this jagged, craggy peak is considered a rite of passage for any aspiring mountaineer. Skiers get a glimpse of the dark, pointed pinnacle of the Grand as they exit the tram and click into their skis.

It was February 2016, and I was with two of my sons, ages seventeen and fourteen, for their February school vacation. They were huddled together a few feet away, ignoring me and trying to catch a glimpse of the mountain through a foggy Plexiglas window. We'd run into Jimmy a few minutes earlier in the tram line. This was the first time I'd seen him in almost a year.

"Of course," I whispered back. "What's up?"

Jimmy leaned in until his face was a few inches from mine. His eyes grew wide. "The Hon is going to solo El Cap this fall," he said.

"What? You're messing with me, right?"

"I swear."

I looked around to see if anyone had overheard, but everyone was grooving to the music that was blasting from a speaker overhead. Jimmy stared back at me, his mouth hanging open.

"He told you?" I asked.

"Yeah. Chai and I are making a film about it. The only people who know about this have all signed nondisclosure agreements, which means we are not allowed to talk about it, so please keep it on the down-low." Elizabeth "Chai" Vasarhelyi is Jimmy's wife, and, like him, she's an award-winning documentary filmmaker. Jimmy and I had known each other for more than fifteen years and had been on many expeditions together, so I wasn't surprised he was letting me in on his secret. Oftentimes, I would write the stories of our expeditions and Jimmy would take the photos, so we made a good team.

"Is he doing Freerider?" I asked, referring to the route up El Capitan that is composed of complex crack systems on the southwest face of the wall. It is a merciless mix of height and steepness that takes even the most experienced climbers several days to complete.

"Yep."

"When?"

"Probably in early November."

As the reality of what I had just been told sunk in, the core of my body quivered. *El Capitan—the world's most majestic cliff. Without a rope. Whoa.*

I had climbed Freerider. Or, I should say, I had attempted it. I got to the top after several days of brutal effort, but not before the climb spit me off several times. And most importantly, I had ropes and protective equipment arresting each fall. On a few of the hardest parts, the cruxes, I simply couldn't hang on to the fingertip jams, and my hands would slip from the flaring cracks. I had been forced to use "aid," meaning I hung on mechanical devices I slotted into cracks in the rock. I cheated. Freerider got its name because it's a "free" climb, which means it can be ascended with nothing more than your hands and feet, but climbers use a rope and harness to act only as a safety net, in case they slip off. The very best can scale Freerider without aid, but I couldn't think of a single person who hadn't fallen at least once on the way up.

So what in the world was Alex Honnold, affectionately known as "the Hon," thinking? El Capitan is three thousand feet of sheer, gleaming, glacier-polished wall. And he planned to attempt it alone. Untethered. No equipment. No fail-safe. Hoping for precision in each grab, in each step. One slip, a toe placed a centimeter too high, a shoe angled off a few degrees, a hold grabbed with the wrong hand—and Alex would plummet through the air as the ground rushed upward at 120 miles per hour. If he fell off the Boulder Problem—which is the hardest section of the entire route—2,100 feet up the side of the wall, he could be in the air for as long as fourteen seconds—about the time it would take me to run the length of a football field.

A young Alex Honnold on the flanks of Mount Kinabalu. This was Honnold's first international climbing expedition.

I knew it was Alex's dream to be the first to free solo El Capitan—I just never thought it would actually happen. When I took him on his first international expedition to Borneo in 2009, he confided in me that he had been thinking about it. Borneo, a large island in Southeast Asia's Malay Archipelago, offered a new kind of big wall terrain and demanded a different kind of climbing than Alex had ever experienced. Borneo proved to be a good stepping-stone on Alex's path toward a ropeless ascent of El Capitan. In the ensuing years, Alex joined me on more climbing expeditions to Chad, Newfoundland, and Oman. Along the way, I witnessed many classic "Alexisms," like him explaining at the base of the wall in Borneo why he didn't climb with a helmet, even on dangerously loose rock (he didn't own one), or the time in Chad's Ennedi Plateau that he sat yawning and examining his cuticles while Jimmy and I faced down four knife-wielding bandits (he thought they were little kids). Perhaps the most classic Alexism of all occurred below a 2,500-foot sea cliff in Oman, when he strapped our rope to his back and told me that he'd stop when he thought it was "appropriate to rope up," and instead climbed the entire way without ever even looking back to see how I was doing.

But Alex and I also spent countless hours talking about philosophy, religion, science, literature, the environment, and his dream to free solo a certain cliff. I often played his foil, especially when it came to the subject of risk. It's not that I'm against the idea of free soloing—I do it myself on occasion. I just wanted Alex to think about how close he was treading to the edge. At times, it occurred to me there were lessons he just hadn't learned yet, like in Borneo when he realized, the hard way, why a helmet is a good thing. Like most climbers, I had an unwritten list of the people who seemed to be pushing it too hard—and Alex Honnold was at the top. By the time I met him, most of the other folks on my list had already met an early demise (and the rest weren't far behind). I liked Alex, and it didn't seem like there were many people willing to call him out, so I felt okay playing the role of father figure. And Alex didn't seem to mind. In fact, it seemed like he enjoyed engaging me on the topic of risk. What it all came down to was that for Alex Honnold, a life lived less than fully is a fate worse than dying—a point on which I wholeheartedly agreed.

I looked over at my two sons still peering through the tram window, eager to ski. Alex was only twenty-nine years old. If he allowed himself to live many more years, he might have more things outside of himself to exist for; presumably his desire for risk would diminish in kind—as it had for me.

But most of all, I wondered what I should do now that Jimmy had burdened me with the knowledge of what was happening. Should I try to talk him out of it? Could I? Or should I support this mad idea and help my friend achieve his dream?

"I think I want to write about this," I said to Jimmy as our gloved fists connected. I had quickly decided that it wasn't my place to try to stop Alex. And if it were one of my children committing to a challenge like this, I'd try to have the same respect for their decision. It would be hard, but I'd try.

"Yeah, I figured. I'll call you," said Jimmy, jabbing his poles into the snow and pushing off. A few seconds later, he disappeared into the gloom.

When Jimmy and I spoke that day in the tram, it had been about a year since he and Chai had debuted *Meru*, the first film they codirected. *Meru* tells the story of a last great problem of Himalayan climbing called the Shark's Fin that Jimmy, Conrad Anker, and Renan Ozturk finally solved in 2011. Jimmy, with Chai's help, had turned *Meru* into a mainstream smash hit. It won the audience choice award at the Sundance Film Festival, was shortlisted for an Oscar, and finished as the highest grossing documentary in 2015.

Hollywood had discovered Jimmy and Chai, and now companies like Sony, Universal, and 21st Century Fox wanted to know what they were doing next. Jimmy was intrigued with the idea of making a film about Alex, the world's greatest free soloist, but he had hesitations about putting Alex in a position where he might feel pressure to perform because he was in front of a camera. And that was before he knew that Alex was thinking about soloing the most important cliff in the world.

Jimmy talked to Chai about the possibility of Alex being the subject of their next film, and they decided that she should call Alex to size him up and ascertain if he had enough depth to hold together a feature-length documentary. It was during this call that Alex mentioned, ever so casually, that he might want to free solo El Capitan. Chai isn't a climber, so the significance of what Alex had just said didn't immediately register.

"When Chai told me about El Cap, I backed right off," Jimmy told me. "That's when I knew that I really didn't want to make the film. When you live in this world and you see the aftermath . . . dying isn't that glorious." For the next two months, he hardly slept.

A lot had to happen. A lot had already happened. This is the story of what led up to an impossible climb. To understand what Alex was planning to attempt, you need to know some things about how he lived and the world that he grew up in. It's a climbing world. Not everyone lives in it, and it's not perfect. But I'm happy, even proud, to say I still do. I guess you could say that I've been lucky that my path in life happened to intersect with Alex Honnold and Jimmy Chin and with a whole bunch of other people who helped lay the foundation for what came next.

Alex was going to climb beyond himself—beyond all of us.

CHAPTER TWO

Understanding Yosemite Decimal System

Before getting into the action-packed drama of climbing some of the most difficult and beautiful cliffs in the world, it's important to review a few of the basics. One of the first things a new climber learns is the numerical system used to grade the difficulty of routes. There are several different systems in use throughout the world, but the American version is called the Yosemite Decimal System (YDS). It categorizes terrain into five classes.

Class 1: A hiking scramble to a rocky gradient; generally hands are not needed.

Class 2: Some scrambling is involved, in which the climber uses both their hands and feet. All but the most inexperienced and clumsy will be able to do a Class 2 without a rope.

Class 3: Simple climbing or scrambling with frequent use of hands. There may be moderate risk of a dangerous fall, and so a rope should be available.

Class 4: Intermediate climbing abilities are required, and most climbers want a rope because of exposure. Falling could be serious or fatal.

Class 5: Climbing always involves a rope and anchors to protect the leader if they fall. One person leads and the other, known as the "second," follows behind, belayed from above, removing the gear along the way.

The 5 before the decimal point of a technical difficulty grade simply denotes that it is Class 5 (roped climbing). Every climb discussed in this book is Class 5, and you'll see them referenced as 5.9, 5.10, 5.10a, and so on. In the 1950s, when the Sierra Club first developed the system, the fifth class included ten sub-grades from zero to nine, denoted as 5.0, 5.1, 5.2, etc. The 5.0 grade was assigned to the easiest fifth-class climb, and 5.9 was given to the hardest, which at the time was a route at Tahquitz Rock in Southern California called Open Book. However, it quickly became apparent that a closed-ended system was not going to work, because soon someone did a climb harder than Open Book, and then another climber bested that effort. So the system was revised and made open-ended. Then climbers began parsing the higher sub-grades into easy, medium, and hard. For instance, 5.10 had three additional sub-divisions: 5.10-, 5.10, and 5.10+. Eventually the plusses and minuses gave way to four increments of a, b, c, and d. Thus, 5.11a is only one tick harder than 5.10d and three ticks—or letter grades—less difficult than 5.11d. (In some cases, climbers have sliced it even thinner, e.g., 5.11b/c.) Freerider, the route up El Capitan that Alex free soloed, according to the exact variation he followed, is rated 5.13a.

It's important to know that climbing grades are inherently subjective. A tall person might be able to reach past a featureless section to a beefy handhold, where a shorter climber may have to make creative use of faint ripples in the rock while stabbing desperately for the same hold. But over time, a consensus develops around a particular climb's difficulty, and the system is remarkably consistent from one climbing area to the next.

Currently, the hardest sport climb in the world is a route called Silence in the Hanshelleren Cave in Flatanger, Norway. The climb was first envisioned and bolted by Adam Ondra in 2012, but it wasn't until 2016 that he began projecting the route in earnest. The bolts are spaced a body length or two apart, which means he'd fall anywhere from ten to thirty feet when the climb spat him off—something that happened hundreds of times. He finally found success, after some fifty days of working the route, in September of 2017. Ondra has tentatively rated the climb 9c, which translates to 5.15d.

So how difficult is a 5.15d? The YouTube video of the first ascent is worth watching. Ondra clings like an insect to an overhanging rock wall, angling out from the bottom of the cliff 30 or 40 degrees beyond vertical. For some reason, he climbs feetfirst, twisting his shoes into a flaring crack over his head. At the crux he winds himself into a Houdini-like contortion so extreme it's a marvel he doesn't tear his body apart. In the video's voice-over, you can hear Ondra joking that he actually used his own arm as a foothold. Higher up, he springs from one tiny hold to the next, going momentarily weightless, then catching himself, barely, with the tips of his fingers each time. After a sequence of several such moves in succession he reaches a larger edge, about the thickness of typical window trim casing, where he "rests," steeling himself for the upper half of the climb, which features similar acrobatics.

CHAPTER THREE
What Happens When You Die?

I grew up in Wellesley, Massachusetts, home to the prestigious all-women's institution Wellesley College and beautiful, sparsely built neighborhoods. Garrison colonials with manicured lawns lined the neighborhood streets, and there were a multitude of beautiful parks and green spaces. Village streets filled with restaurants and small local shops gave Wellesley the feel of a small New England town. Despite the regular bustle of commuters to and from Boston and the often competitive nature of its residents to be the best and the brightest, it was an idyllic place to live. As a kid, I basically lived on my bike, but I also played Little League baseball and soccer, and I ski raced on the weekends in New Hampshire. My parents gave me my introduction to the outdoors, but they both had a hands-off parenting style, and they let me roam free in our neighborhood and beyond.

Growing up, I adored animals. One day when I was about ten years old, I rolled home on my bike to find an injured bird in my backyard. I named the bird Sam. With a nest made from an old shoebox, I nursed him back to health with birdseed mixed with peanut butter in a little dish filled with water. With some sidewalk chalk, I recorded Sam's daily progress on the walkway leading to the back door of our house. After a week or so, I went to the garage one morning to check on him. To my horror, I found that the door had been left open a crack and some creature, probably a cat, had gotten ahold of my little bird friend. There was nothing left behind but a few feathers. I was heartbroken and angry. And I couldn't bear the thought that it might have been me who had forgotten to close the door.

After Sam's death my head was spinning. I had so many unanswered questions. One day I approached my father as he was sitting in the sunroom of our home reading *The New York Times* and simply asked, "What happens when you die?"

He lowered his paper and looked me in the eye. "You're worm food, Mark." Snapping his paper back into place, he went back to his reading, just like that, as I stood there dumbfounded.

That night, while lying in bed, I turned the brief conversation over and over in my ten-year-old mind. If there's nothing on the other side, I reasoned, if heaven and hell are figments of our collective imaginations, then death must be absolute. Worm food. Forever.

From that moment on, the question of what I was supposed to do with my limited time on earth consumed me. I was determined to figure out how to live my life to the fullest while I had the chance. My most meaningful days were the ones I spent having fun with my friends. Looking back all these years later, I'm struck by the fact that the things that have given meaning to my life have never really changed. As I got older, my playground shifted from the hills of New England to some of the wildest peaks in the world, but I always stayed true to my core principle, which was simply to squeeze as much juice as I could from the game that we call life.

▲▲

It was in this restless period of my life that I came to idolize Evel Knievel, an American stunt performer and entertainer who rose to fame between 1965 and 1980 for his death-defying motorcycle jumps. Known as the "King of the Daredevils" or the "Godfather of Extreme Sports," his white jumpsuit gave him the look of a real-life superhero, and his image was plastered on posters and lunch boxes for children everywhere to see. He managed over seventy-five death-defying motorcycle jumps in his career. My dad bought me a windup Evel on his stunt bike, and I spent hours launching the plastic superhero off elaborate ramps that I'd set up across our house. I made them out of discarded shoeboxes and shingles, and I'd crash the windup toy into houseplants and toy soldiers. When he was three years old, my son got a Duke Caboom toy, a character from *Toy Story 4* whose persona is undoubtedly a nod to the original American legend.

Evel Knievel jumping the fountains at Caesars Palace in Las Vegas on December 31, 1967.

I gravitated toward Evel Knievel with no hesitation and soon moved from playing with a toy inside the house to setting up my own stunts across the neighborhood. On a long, unused dirt driveway behind the home of some senior citizens, my friends and I used two-by-fours and plywood to build a ten-foot-high ramp-to-ramp jump. The ramps were about twice our height and prone to collapsing when we hit them at high speed on our bikes. I crashed so many times on my home-built ramps, and required so many stitches, that one might have thought I was trying to meet or exceed the 433 broken bones that Evel Knievel sustained throughout his life—a feat that landed him in the *Guinness Book of World Records*.

I wasn't looking to make a mark or to be famous. My motivations were far simpler than that. I just hated being bored, and I was always looking for a way to spice things up. One day I happened to notice that the water-struck bricks forming the exterior of my house made for perfect finger holds, and for the next several weeks I spent every spare moment I had exploring the climbing potential of my house! I fell off on occasion, but I got good at the "tuck and roll," as I called it. I was young and my body was tough and springy, and somehow, I never got seriously hurt. Maybe I was lucky or maybe I had an uncommon knack for always landing in the right way, or for not tripping or screwing up at the wrong moment. But because I never suffered a bad outcome for my actions, apart from those stitches (which I did, admittedly, get a lot of), it was hard not to want to continually outdo myself. Just like Evel, I continued to try new things and go bigger and bigger, because why not? It was a constant test of myself and a way to bond and have some laughs with my friends. If I had to go back, I wouldn't change the way I was, because my spirit came from the heart, and it lay right at the core of who I was as a person. But now, as a father of four, I will say that I would never permit my children to do the things I did when I was a kid.

One thing I did learn is that none of it was very fun when I was alone. The joy came from sharing the experience of hooting and hollering, the excitement of pulling off a new trick, with my friends. What I didn't realize until I was older was that deep down, I wanted/needed that same support and recognition I was getting from my friends from my parents too—especially my dad. I suppose that I hoped my friends and their zeal for my stunts would fill the void that my relationship with my parents had left.

My discovery of risk-taking as a cure for boredom guided me to long friendships with people who more or less shared this habit. But some of my young friends often opted out of joining me, and in hindsight, they were smart to do so and avoid getting in trouble—or worse, hurt.

One day, while I was rooting around in my father's den, I found a box of fancy wooden matches with gold tips that he must have picked up on one of his business trips. I had a clandestine site in the woods behind my house where I would set fire to everything from candles and birch bark to bottle rockets and fireworks, so I put the matches in my pocket for later.

At the bus stop the next morning, I held up one of my new treasures between my fingers. The kids from my neighborhood gazed at it in awe. I was doing what I always did, trying to get their attention and to light them up with curiosity and excitement.

"Is that real gold?" asked one of them.

"Of course," I replied.

"Can I have one?" he asked.

The bus stop was next to a small, shallow, scum-filled pond. It was early winter, and a thin layer of ice covered the black muddy water. There was a Styrofoam coffee cup bobbing in the ice about fifty yards from shore.

"Get that cup," I told him, "and this thing is yours."

Seconds later, he was off, breaking the ice with his fists as he half swam, half waded through the freezing swampy water. He didn't make it to school that day, but he got the match—and became the first of the "Golden Fellows."

For the next couple of weeks, the gold-tipped matches kept my friends motivated as we completed the next important mission that I'd laid out for us—to dance on the chimney of every house in the neighborhood. It was a dangerous and misguided plan, but we laughed and whooped every time one my friends successfully climbed to the top of a typically snowy roof and did his *Solid Gold* celebration dance on or above its ridge. The boy would scramble down with a grin splashed across his face and accept his prize. I'd make a ceremony of the presentation of the Golden Match in the middle of the icy night.

When I handed out the final golden-tipped match, it was like the Once-ler felling the last Truffula tree in *The Lorax*—everyone packed up and went home. But there were still several houses left on the list, so I went on alone, scaling drainpipes, going hand over hand across gutters, and friction-climbing up slate roofs. But it just wasn't the same dancing my little jigs on top of people's houses without anybody watching and cheering me on.

I started coming up with schemes at a young age before I had any mentors to lead me in an alternative direction. To me, it seemed like the best way to get the most out of life with my newfound knowledge that I had a finite amount of time on this planet. I wanted to continue to keep things exciting, to feel as though I was making the most of my time on earth with whatever talents I had, just as Alex did later in his own life.

CHAPTER FOUR
"Crazy Kids of America"

Every Friday afternoon my mom pushed my sister and me into the back of our lemon-colored Chrysler station wagon and we drove from the suburbs into Boston to pick up my dad in the parking garage of the bank where he worked. My dad always took the wheel from there for the three-hour drive up to our vacation house in New Hampshire's White Mountains. My sister, Amy, and I slid around in the back seat, keeping the boredom at bay by annoying each other however we could.

One of my favorite ways to torment Amy was with a move I called the "ear flick." I'd wait until she wasn't paying attention, and then quick as a flash I'd give her earlobe a flick with my thumb and forefinger. Another all-time favorite (of mine, not hers) was a move I named the "Barbwick." When my parents weren't looking, I'd press my palm to the hairline above her forehead and pull backward, stretching her forehead and raising her eyebrows, which never failed to give her face a look of surprise.

In New Hampshire, I employed similar antics and used the Golden Fellows model to start a new club called Crazy Kids of America with my ski-racing buddies. The club included some now noteworthy characters like Tyler Hamilton, a compact ball of energy who always had a sly sparkle in his eye

Crazy Kids of America, circa 1982. Top row, left to right: Paul Getchell, Muffy Arndt, Jeff Chapman, Scott Fitzgerald, the author, Bruce Barry, Ben Barr, unknown. Bottom row, left to right: Jesse McAleer, Amy Synnott, Robert Frost, Tyler Hamilton, Tyler Vadenboncouer.

and who'd go on to become Lance Armstrong's right-hand man in the Tour de France, and Rob Frost, who is now a high-angle cameraman and film-maker. Even Chris Davenport, the legendary extreme skier, joined us for the occasional mission; his catlike athletic ability and rambunctious daredevil spirit made him a perfect fit for our crew.

As the leader of the group, I always had an array of challenges with which to test my recruits. These tests ranged from simple things like eating disgusting concoctions put together with cafeteria condiments to walking out on thin ice to fetch various items, risking icy submersion. Our specialty was pole vaulting across ice-choked rivers with bamboo ski gates that we'd "borrow" from our ski team lodge at Wildcat Mountain, and these missions always followed a similar routine. We became highly skilled vaulters, propelling ourselves across fifteen-foot spans of water. Of course, one had to pick the sturdiest gates from the supply, otherwise you'd get stuck with leftover bamboo poles that were flimsy and prone to snapping in half, typically right when you're hovering over the frosty riffles and about to fall in.

"You've totally got this, dude," I'd call out to a would-be jumper from the far side of the river, rubbing my hands together in anticipation of a magnificent failure.

Many of my fellow Crazy Kids took what we called the "Nestea Plunge," our name for what happened when you failed spectacularly and plunged into the icy water. A new recruit once showed up and proceeded to attempt a varsity-level pole vault from an ice-slicked rock over the most turbulent section of the river—wearing his ski boots, rather than the insulated foam Moon Boots the rest of us wore. We knew it was sheer folly to shoot for such a big jump in clunky plastic boots, but who were we to stop him if he wanted to try? He missed badly, of course, and completely disappeared underwater. He resurfaced a short distance downstream, and, like the good Crazy Kid that he was, scrapped his way back to shore.

Our ski coaches pretended they were unaware of their team's extracurricular activities, but they must have noticed the rapidly dwindling supply of ski gates and our banter about who had been the most daring that day. And in a show of tacit approval, at the end of the season banquet they let me give out my own Crazy Kids of America awards. Each member got a cardboard Burger King crown with our logo pasted on it—a hand-drawn pencil rendering of a kid pole vaulting over a river. I occasionally handed out parachute men too, which we saved to later launch off the top of Cathedral Ledge, a five-hundred-foot cliff in nearby North Conway, New Hampshire.

Most of the parents appreciated my contribution to New Hampshire youth culture, live free or die and all that, but a few of them thought I was reckless and a bad influence. At least one kid, after taking the Nestea Plunge and going home near hypothermic, was forbidden from participating in our club's activities. Looking back, they were absolutely right to be worried, and I can't blame any parent who decided their son or daughter would be better off hanging out with a different crew. As a kid, I never stopped to think about the possible repercussions of any of our stunts or actions, and I had no role model, outside of a professional daredevil, to show me how to do things differently. We were simply trying to get the most out of life the only way we knew how in the surroundings we were given. And this spirit, however misguided it may have sometimes appeared, is the same spirit that still drives me to explore the world and to take the harder path whenever I come to a fork in the road. It's only now, as I am older with four children of my own, that I realize how lucky we got most of the time—how things so easily could have gone wrong. Ironically, it was my discovery of climbing a few years later that slowly taught me to how to accomplish my goals in a precise and strategic way, in a setting where there was no room for error, and sometimes, no second chances.

CHAPTER FIVE
First Cathedral Climb

Everything I knew about rock climbing I had gleaned from a poster my dad hung on the wall in my bedroom. The poster was a photo of a craggy-jawed man hanging by his fingertips from the lip of an overhang, suspended in midair with nothing but a skinny rope tied around his waist. It never occurred to me why my dad had bought it; in my mind he was a boring banker who enjoyed outdoor pursuits like skiing and hiking, but he wasn't one to push boundaries. No one had told me that it was a vintage poster from the earliest days of the sport, before the invention of harnesses, carabiners, and kernmantle ropes. And I didn't ask.

The poster was my only how-to manual. I had never rock climbed before, and I didn't know anyone personally who had tried it either, but our vacation house in Jackson, New Hampshire, was fatefully located just a few miles from the world-class crag called Cathedral Ledge, where I had launched my parachute men as a kid.

One summer weekend when I was fifteen years old, I convinced my close friend Jeff Chapman to join me on this endeavor. At the time, I was blissfully unaware of the profound effect that day would have on the future trajectory of my life. Since Jeff and I were too young to have our licenses, we asked my dad for a ride to the cliff, and fifteen minutes later he pulled up in the parking area where we caught our first view of the vertical wall of granite through an opening in the towering pine trees that lined the base of Cathedral Ledge.

Perhaps it was the tightly laced Converse Chuck Taylors on my feet, or the hardware store white utility rope neatly coiled over my shoulder, or the fact that my frequent partner in crime and fellow Crazy Kid stood by my side, but for once, my dad—who had an uncanny knack for failing to observe much of anything—realized that something was up.

"Hey," he called over, his arm hanging out the window of the K-car. "What exactly are you guys planning to do here?"

"Oh, nothing much," I replied. "Don't worry about us. Just come back in a few hours to pick us up."

My dad gave the scene a good hard look, then slapped the wood-paneled door twice. "Okay," he said. "You boys have fun." And that was it. We were off on our own with nothing except an old poster image in my mind and a cliff ahead of us.

athedral Ledge, a five-hundred-foot granite cliff in North Conway, New Hampshire, where the author cut his teeth as a young climber.

▲▲

For our first rock climb we chose a mossy gully in the center of the wall. With its ample supply of trees and vegetation, it appeared an ideal route to the summit. Before starting off, Jeff and I established our cardinal rule: the leader must not fall. It was simple, even obvious perhaps, but it made sense to us. We decided that whoever followed behind should have the security of the rope being held from above. This way, only one person had to risk their life.

We took turns clawing our way up through the loose rock and vegetation, and when the rope ran out, we would untie it, give it a couple loops around a tree, then use the friction against the bark to provide security for the second climber. The higher we climbed, the steeper the wall became, until we stood on either side of a stout hemlock growing from a matrix of hard-packed dirt, moss, and rusty beer cans. Above us loomed the crux pitch, a vertical wall of loose blocks stacked on top of each other like a life-sized game of Jenga.

It was Jeff's turn to lead, but he wasn't sure he was up for it. I certainly wanted nothing to do with the crumbling wall that hung above us. By this point I had become a bit of a master at persuading kids to do dangerous things, and Jeff was not immune to my charms. I enticed him with an extra Crazy Kids award, and this seemed to be all the motivation he needed. A few minutes later, he was several body lengths above me, clinging to a mossy house of cards. When he reached over his head for a grip in a horizontal crack, a television-sized flake shifted, raining pebbles and dirt down the wall onto my head. "I think I'm going to fall," he cried out.

The author climbing a granite aqueduct in his hometown of Wellesley, Massachusetts, in 1988 at age seventeen.

"Hold on a second," I called up, untying from the rope and then using it to lash myself to the hemlock. After several turns around the trunk, I locked the end off with a series of half hitches, knots I'd learned to tie by trial and error. Satisfied there was no way I was going anywhere should he come hurtling down, I called up to Jeff something obnoxious like, "Okay, you can fall now."

Jeff looked down between his legs and saw me lashed to the tree. Two things were clear: if he fell, he was going to die (or at least be badly mangled)—and I wasn't. Something about this situation seemed to violate our honor code, and the injustice of me not bleeding and broken by his side at the base of the cliff inspired him to pull it together and climb back down.

As we scrabbled our way down the gully, still determined to ascend the cliff, I noticed a horizontal break that offered a potential traverse out onto the main face. We followed it, scrambling sideways, clawing our way hand over hand through bushes to reach a small ledge about two hundred feet above the ground, with sweeping walls of clean granite surrounding it in every direction. Still tied together with the clothesline, each with some extra coils over our shoulders, we sat side by side, taking in the bird's-eye view of the valley far below us. We gave each other a knowing look. We had taken Crazy Kids of America to a whole new level—and it felt so right.

Our reverie was cut short by a jangly, metallic sound, and a few seconds later a hand appeared at the lip below our feet, followed by a man who hauled himself onto our ledge. What followed was a moment of mutual disbelief as the two climbing parties took each other in. He was probably in his twenties, bearded, with calloused fingers and taut, muscular arms. I stared at his collection of space-age-looking gadgets that hung from snap links on a bandolier over his shoulder. His rope—unlike ours, which was composed of three lumpy braids—had a smooth sheath decorated in a vibrant print of yellow-and-black geometric patterns.

"Wow, that's some nice-looking gear you've got," I said.

The fit man stared back at us, his face all surprise, and said something like, "How in the world did you two get up here?"

Jeff and I scooted out of his way and observed with rapt attention as he secured himself to some bolts in the wall with a couple of snap links that he unhooked from his harness. "We should get our hands on some of those for next time," I said to Jeff.

When the climber's friend arrived and saw us sitting next to his partner, he was equally bewildered. But the climbers wasted no time feeding their ropes through some rings in the wall and setting up what I would learn was a rappel. I keenly observed their every move, secretly hoping that our new friends might have a word of advice for our descent, or better yet, help us get down. I was frozen in awe of their abilities and wanted so badly to be able to do this myself that I didn't ask for their help. Lowering myself down on a rope looked like a great option, but as I watched them set their gear up, I realized that it would be tricky without harnesses, their snap links, or those fancy friction-plate thingies they were now feeding their ropes into. At the very least I wanted some kudos from them, a word or two acknowledging that we climbers were all cut from the same cloth.

But instead, as nonchalant about our fate as my dad had been that morning, they stepped off the edge onto the steep, smooth rock wall below. They slid down their ropes, leaving us kids alone on the ledge to figure out our own way down.

After they hit the ground below, they pulled their ropes out of the anchor by our heads, leaving them empty. We fed our clothesline through the rings, just like we'd seen them do. Since we didn't have any gear other than the rope, the only option was a Batman-style bare-handed rappel, which worked for me until I reached the end of the rope and found myself dangling in the middle of a blank wall, still a hundred feet above the ground. Thankfully, using my feet to push off, I was able to pendulum swing over into the gully. Jeff followed suit. From there it was an easy down climb back to solid ground.

▲▲

My Chuck Taylors had performed admirably on Cathedral Ledge, but now that I was a real rock climber, I needed to start dressing the part. This time, I turned to my mom for help, and she took me to Olkens, the local sporting goods store.

I sat on the shoe-fitting stool, my arms crossed cockily, my head still spinning from my recent near conquest of Cathedral Ledge. As I scanned the store and observed the other customers, I wondered if they'd ever experienced what it felt like to cling to the side of a cliff hundreds of feet in the air, like I just had.

Helped by a rather officious shoe salesman and my doting mom, I tried a couple pairs until we found the perfect fit. I wore the shoes home, and as soon as we arrived, I jumped on my bike and raced over to a rock in the woods called the Bates Boulder. The moment I stepped off the ground, I could immediately feel what a difference it made to be a wearing a "rock shoe." It wasn't just the way the sole gripped the rock, which was heavenly, but the way the shoe looked on my foot when I gazed down at it from above. I was in love.

After bouldering around for half an hour, another climber showed up—a blond-haired kid from my neighborhood who went to private school. I didn't know him that well. He sat down and laced up his own rock boots, then hopped onto the boulder and started climbing next to me.

"Check out these new rock shoes," I bragged as we hung a few feet apart from each other. But when he gazed down at my feet, a bemused smile lit his face.

"Those are hiking boots," he scoffed. "These," he continued, gesturing to the sleek-looking boots on his own feet, "are rock climbing shoes."

I immediately jumped off the rock and looked down at my feet in disgust. In my fit of embarrassment, I wanted to throw my toys, to tell him he was wrong, but deep down, I knew he was right. "The owner of Olkens is going to be hearing about this," I said as I jumped on my bike and began pedaling furiously toward home.

While my mom worked on correcting the mistake we had made, I set my sights on a few of the other items I needed for my rock climbing kit, namely a harness and some of those snap links. The latter was easy, because a friend's brother had done an experiential multiweek outdoor program, Outward Bound, and he had walked away with two snap links, which we soon learned were called carabiners. Chuck, like most younger brothers, had combed every inch of his big bro's room when he wasn't around, so he knew exactly where he had stashed them in his closet.

Somewhere along the way my friends and I figured out that the webbing used to make harnesses is the same material as seat belts in cars. This was fortuitous, because I had recently spied a burned-out abandoned Volkswagen Bug in an industrial area near the subway line in Boston. The seat belts, it turned out, were the one part of the car that were still intact. We cut them free with a buck knife.

Rock shoes: check.

Snap links: check.

Harnesses: check.

All that was missing now was a proper rope. My mom was a garage sale fanatic, and she frequently brought me with her. Most of the stuff at our house came from these garage sales, including my massive owl collection, which my mom had started for me because she loved owls—even though I didn't. She looked stunned when early one Saturday morning, I asked over my bowl of Frosted Mini-Wheats if she would take me to yard sales that day, and then, when that yielded nothing, again the following weekend, and the weekend after. And it was then, in the driveway of a ranch house in the next town over, picking over card tables covered with piles of a deceased person's tchotchkes and packages of half-used batteries and old appliances, that I found the rope—120 feet of super-stiff braided "goldline." I knew it wasn't quite like the rope the guys had on Cathedral Ledge, but it was clearly unquestionably strong. My mom gave the man a few bucks, and it was mine.

Rope: check.

So despite still not having any coaching or people around me to learn from, I began to take steps to becoming an actual bona fide rock climber.

I was delighted to discover that the Wellesley Free Library had a climbing and mountaineering section. I'd been rooting around in this library since I was a little kid, and all those years this treasure trove had been sitting right under my nose: *The Vertical World of Yosemite* by Galen A. Rowell, *The Freedom of the Hills* by the Mountaineers, *Climbing Ice* by Yvon Chouinard, *The White Spider* by Heinrich Harrer, *The Six Mountain-Travel Books* by Eric Shipton, *Annapurna* by Maurice Herzog, and *The Shining Mountain* by Peter Boardman. I signed them out and greedily read them in quick succession. These books and others opened my eyes to an unknown world of high adventure, to a time frame the authors referred to as "the golden age" of climbing and exploration. The golden age, from what I read, was a time when there were still blanks on the map, when all the great mountains of the world were unclimbed and any person who had the courage, the resolve, the tenacity, could go stick a flag in a place on planet Earth where no person had ever been.

In the leaf of *The Shining Mountain* was a picture of a bearded Joe Tasker hanging in a hammock suspended on the side of a frozen vertical wall of white Himalayan granite called Changabang, a glacier thousands of dizzying feet below. I stared at that picture for days until I could just about feel the cold stone against my back, the nylon pinching my shoulders, a cold wind frosting my face. Far more than the summit, I became enthralled with the idea of the bivouac, the part of these epic climbs when you get to relax, when maybe you'd had a decent meal and were warmly ensconced in your sleeping bag, comfy and secure in the midst of a thin-aired, cold, cold world of rock and ice. I had different role models all of a sudden. Evel Knievel and his short-lived stunts were taking a back seat to a world that suddenly made sense to me. The puzzle of how to unlock the secrets to get up new rock faces appealed to my mind and my sense of adventure. The physical moves on the rock suited me, and I didn't think about any of the potential consequences at the time. The risk factor was drowned out by the deafening call to exploration. It seemed simple. If I did it right, and I worked hard at it, I could do what these people were doing, and beyond.

There was one mountain that stood out like a beacon among all the rest—the Trango Tower, located in Pakistan. I first gazed upon its other-worldliness while sitting at a carrel desk in a back room of the library. This ethereal spire rising into the mist knitted perfectly with my vision of what a mountain should be. One day . . .

And there, in that musty reading room, a trajectory was firmly set. The path I embarked on took me to peaks and places where I was able to challenge my own psychological and physical limits as well as the assumptions of what many thought was possible in the sport of big wall climbing and global exploration. I could never have guessed this path would eventually intersect with that of another dreamer, a kid with similar boundless energy and determination and a restless mind, and who wouldn't even be born for another fifteen years.

CHAPTER SIX
What He Was Born to Do

Alex Honnold's mother, Dierdre, claims that he could already stand up eleven hours after he was born. "You know when they grab on to your pinkies . . . you hold on, he would stand up. How many babies can do that?" His hands were so big that people couldn't help but comment on them when first meeting him as a baby. While Dierdre describes Alex as a kid who had a huge heart and someone who was always thoughtful of others and eerily intuitive about things that should have been beyond his years, she also says that he was a difficult child, mainly because he just never stopped moving. As a baby, he regularly climbed out of his crib, and no high chair could contain him. At the playground, he used to annoy other parents because he was constantly climbing trees, walls, and jungle gyms, and when the other kids tried to follow him, they'd often fall and get hurt. When he was three years old, he'd go to bed when he wanted to (not when his parents told him to), which typically was not until ten thirty or eleven at night. Nonetheless, he'd be up at four a.m., pulling on his parents' bedsheets, even jumping up and down on their mattress, until they gave in and groggily took him outside to play in the pitch dark. His energy was limitless. Any toys he had at his disposal were often used in unorthodox ways. Instead of playing with a toy guitar or building something with blocks, he would use these items as tools in order to help him "get vertical" or to launch himself into the air.

Alex never walked anywhere if he could get there by climbing! This is how he "walked" to the park in Garden City, Long Island, New York.

His mother was always looking for new ways for Alex to use his energy and athletic abilities, and so she signed him up for gymnastics, but Alex ended up excelling to a fault. He performed to a level that was beyond his age group, and his coaches tried to slow him down. Alex was constantly frustrated and quit after two years. It wasn't until Alex was five that he made his first introduction to the sport of climbing.

Alex's mom was writing a travel book entitled *Sacramento with Kids*. The idea was to create a guidebook for families traveling in the area with children. She would test every activity she could find, and if Alex and his sister Stasia enjoyed it, it would make the book. If not, it wouldn't. She'd heard of a new climbing gym opening in a town that was thirty miles away and originally was going to ignore it, because she didn't understand the sport and assumed it would be dangerous. Eventually she decided to check it out and brought both kids with her. While she was interviewing the gym employees for her book, two climbers had taken Alex aside, put him in a harness, and sent him up a wall. Dierdre realized something was up the moment the room went quiet. She turned, and there was her five-year-old son at the top of a forty-foot wall, being cheered by every person in the gym.

Another five years went by before a gym opened in Sacramento, the Honnolds' hometown. Sometimes his father would take him, but Alex often biked the ten miles to the gym alone. He started to enter competitions, and it was mainly his father who accompanied him to offer support while his mother worked or stayed with Stasia.

When Alex was eleven, he got his first taste of outdoor climbing during a family reunion in France. A friend of Dierdre's who was an avid climber took Alex up a three-hundred-foot cliff in the Savoy Alps. According to Diedre's friend, Alex handled it "like it was nothing." She could tell by the size of the smile on his face that this was only the beginning for Alex.

The climbing world first learned of Alex in July 2004, after his first year at the University of California, Berkeley, because of the USA Climbing Sport & Speed Youth National Championships. The competition was held at Pipeworks climbing center in Sacramento, Alex's home gym, where he'd been competing on their team since the gym opened in 2000. Feeding off the energy of the hometown crowd, Alex delivered an inspiring performance and took second place in the youth division (ages fourteen through nineteen). This qualified him for the world championships in Scotland, which were set to take place two months later. But shortly after nationals, Alex's father died at the age of fifty-five from a heart attack while running to catch a flight at the Phoenix airport. He'd served as Alex's one-man support crew for the past eight years, driving him to competitions all over the country and holding his rope for countless hours.

At the world championships later that year, Alex couldn't muster any motivation or enthusiasm for the event because of his dad's recent passing. He underperformed, taking thirty-ninth place.

The thought of another year at UC Berkeley filled Alex with dread, so he asked his mom if he could drop out. She agreed, since she knew how miserable he had been—he had described the college experience to her as "heinous." In high school, he did the bare minimum to get by and didn't have a real passion for academics but managed to be a top student in his school's International Baccalaureate program. Alex had also always been a little socially awkward and didn't put forth much of an effort to make friends. His time at Berkeley didn't seem to be any different.

Climbing was his one salvation, and he hardly ever missed a day. When he wasn't hitting the gym, the local crag Indian Rock, or the stone-clad buildings on the Berkeley campus, he sat around in his boxers playing video games and doing pull-ups on the doorjamb of his room. His classmates, who had little to no awareness of his existence, had no way of knowing that the quiet genius who was flying under everyone's radar was slowly transforming himself into a climber the likes of which the world had never seen.

Alex dropped out of college, and on December 26, 2004, he went for a hike by himself on Mount Tallac. He slipped and fell hundreds of feet over scree and rocks, breaking his wrist along the way and hitting his head so hard he could barely call his mother for help. He happened to have brought his new cell phone with him, which had been a recent gift from her. There's a good chance he would never have made it off the mountain if he had not had that phone.

Alex recuperated on the couch for only a week. After that, he rode his bike to the climbing gym, where he tentatively tested how it felt to pull on his broken wrist. Just like Evel Knievel, Alex did not want to let an injury get in the way of his climbing. Only his pinky and ring finger stuck out of the cast. It hurt when he pulled himself up the plastic holds with his two weakest fingers, but not enough to stop him. "Should you really be doing that?" people asked. "It's no big deal," Alex would reply. His wrist took months longer to get better than it should have.

He was still climbing indoors on plywood walls covered in textured paint, a medium as far removed from the real world as the landscapes of Azeroth. But the books and magazines on his bedside table showed a whole world beyond indoor climbing where a man could leave his mark. Similar to my days spent in the Wellesley Free Library as a kid, Alex devoured every new issue of *Climbing* and *Rock and Ice* magazines. And like every other climber, he saw that among all of the sport's various disciplines, from indoor climbing to bouldering to high-altitude mountaineering, it was the free soloists like Henry Barber, John Bachar, Peter Croft, and Dean Potter who had the prodigious power to accomplish feats that only a small minority of the climbing community even attempted. To have the genius skill and savvy mind to climb walls without a partner or a rope appealed to Alex. There was also the sheer practicality of not needing a partner, which worked well for Alex. Alex watched videos like *Masters of Stone* over and over, in which these guys climbed into the stratosphere on fairy-tale cliffs, clinging to existence with nothing but a few fingers and a sliver of boot rubber.

One image in particular captured Alex's imagination: a photo of nineteen-year-old John Bachar, without a rope, high off the ground on a steep and slippery Yosemite crack called New Dimensions. The photo, taken in 1976, documents the first 5.11-rated free solo in Yosemite. The fingers on Bachar's left hand are sunk into a crack that splits a soaring vertical open book of rock three hundred feet above the ground. He leans into the left page of the book with his shoulder while his right hand tucks behind his back into his chalk bag. His left toe is boxed in the crack while

John Barchar free soloing New Dimensions in 1982. He first climbed this three-hundred-foot, 5.11-rated route in 1976 but there was no documentation of it. Bachar's ascent of New Dimensions redefined the limits of what was thought possible because, at the time, the hardest roped climbing in Yosemite was only one grade harder.

the right is pasted haphazardly against the opposite wall, blank except for a peppering of black lichen. He wears a pair of white track shorts with blue stripes on the hip and a red long-sleeved collared shirt. His wavy blond hair sticks out from under a backward-facing pinstriped train engineer's cap. A thin mustache traces his firmly closed lips, which are neither smiling nor frowning. Piercing blue eyes look directly into the camera. He appears utterly relaxed and nonchalant, with more than a hint of arrogance in his expression; he stares you down like a street hooligan lounging against a lamppost on his home turf. It's a photo that inspired a generation of climbers. A picture of a man who knows exactly who he is.

CHAPTER SEVEN

Becoming a Soloist

Charlie Honnold named Alex and his sister the beneficiaries of his life insurance policy. Alex's share of the interest on the bonds was about $300 per month, which was just enough to fund the itinerant climbing lifestyle that he envisioned as his escape from living with his mom. He borrowed her old Chevy minivan, loaded it with his climbing gear, a sleeping bag, and a few changes of clothes, and gave his mom a hug. In April 2005 he left home to find out what he was capable of.

In Joshua Tree National Park in Southern California, Alex wandered around the Mojave Desert among the bulbous, egg-shaped rocks looking for things to climb. He wasn't necessarily looking to be a soloist, but he was alone and far too shy to seek out partners in the campground. Soloing was simply the most practical way for Alex to climb when and where he wanted to, and at his own pace.

Things sometimes got weird when he ran into other people. A part of him wanted to show off, but only if the climbing was well within his comfort zone. If the climbing was hard, near the limit of what he was capable of when free soloing a route he had never climbed before, which at the time was 5.10c or so, he couldn't have spectators. One day he was climbing a route that featured a short roof that was high enough off the ground for a fall to be fatal. His hands were jammed into a crack above the overhang and, as he was getting up the nerve to commit to the move, he looked down and saw two tourists staring at him. Alex froze and then retreated to a comfortable stance. He would wait until they left. But the tourists lingered, and Alex found himself wondering whether they were judging him, if they thought he was a coward for his obvious trepidation. Finally, they left, and Alex finished the climb. Later, reflecting on the incident in an essay published in *Rock and Ice* magazine, he wrote: "After that, soloing became even more solitary for me because I feared doing something stupid when people were watching. Yet it was still a difficult balance, since there are always people at climbing areas and I often just wanted to climb. And honestly, sometimes it was nice to impress people. But pride is dangerous since it leads to recklessness or overconfidence, which have no place in soloing."

When the minivan died, Alex kept going on his bicycle. As summer approached, Joshua Tree became too hot for climbing, so he got a ride north to Bishop, on the east side of the Sierra Nevada. He stationed himself in a campground called the Pit. In the morning, he'd ride his bike to the Happy Boulders or to a sport climbing area called the Owens River Gorge. At the latter, Alex spent his days soloing, mostly out of necessity. He still didn't have any partners.

Alex's obsession at the time was to tick off as many routes as he could. His goal was twenty-five pitches a day. A pitch is typically defined as a rope length, but that can vary greatly from sixty feet to 180 feet. He was climbing anywhere from 1,500 to 4,500 vertical feet a day. At night in his tent, he compulsively recorded every climb in his black book. He was on-sighting these routes, climbing them with no previous knowledge or "beta" about the best way to actually get up them. When a kid arrives at a new playground, the features might seem similar, but until you get on it for the first time, you don't know what to expect. He almost always downclimbed rather than topping out over the rim of the gorge and hiking down. Downclimbing is dangerous, but Alex preferred it because going up and over often required negotiating loose, dangerous rock. Most importantly, downclimbing meant that he could count each route twice. He stuck with this program day in and day out in order to climb, as he later put it, "crappy little faces with no appeal besides the tick I could put in my guidebook."

One day he headed up a 5.9 arete—an outside corner as opposed to an inside corner or open book. By now a route of this difficulty felt routine and casual. About twelve feet above the ground he slipped, landing in the dirt with a thud. After he realized he wasn't hurt, he looked around to see if anyone had seen him fall. There was no one in sight. He sat for a few moments contemplating what had just happened. It was his first unexpected fall while free soloing, and it could just as easily have happened higher up the route, high enough for him to be dead. He brushed himself off and went back up. You have to get back on the horse, right?

CHAPTER EIGHT
Yosemite

Yosemite National Park lies about 150 miles due east of San Francisco in the Sierra Nevada Mountains. It encompasses 1,200 square miles, about the size of Rhode Island, most of which is roadless wilderness where intrepid hikers can explore granite domes, snow-clad peaks, and pristine alpine lakes. But many of the park's four million annual visitors skip the backcountry and go straight to Yosemite Valley, a seven-mile-long-by-one-mile-wide glacier-carved vale that lies on the park's southwestern corner at four thousand feet above sea level. Here the tourists clog the loop road and throng to overpriced hotels and crowded campgrounds where the hum of RV generators and squeals of children fill the air.

My first trip to the "Ditch," as climbers call Yosemite Valley, was in 1989. As I emerged from the Wawona Tunnel on Highway 41 and saw the valley for the first time, I nearly crashed my Honda CB650 swerving into the parking lot of the famous overlook called Tunnel View. A few seconds later I was standing on a stone wall, gobsmacked by the panorama that lay before me. It was early May, and the alpine high country above Half Dome, still covered in snow, seemingly floated in the sky on the far end of the valley. Cascades poured down gullies on both sides of the valley, but these were mere trickles compared to the six-hundred-foot Bridalveil Falls that plunged from a tiger-striped wall in the foreground. The floor of the valley was lush green and densely forested. Trees rose up the slope to the edge of the overlook, where two ponderosa pines, sticking up above the rest, framed the view.

I remember taking my time and trying to soak it all in before turning my attention to the titanic cliff that loomed over the north side of the valley directly across from the falls. I had not anticipated how intimidating it would feel to stand face-to-face with El Capitan. If I hadn't spent years dreaming about climbing this wall, I could have simply trembled in awe of its immensity and pondered the retreating Ice Age glaciers that carved it from the earth's bedrock more than ten thousand years ago. But I had long ago decided that scaling El Capitan would be my rite of passage as a climber, and for that reason, the cliff seemed to mock me, as if laughing at my audacity. Ansel Adams took a famous black-and-white photo from Tunnel View back in 1934, and he put it on the cover of his classic book *Yosemite and the Range of Light*. I had studied that photo until I felt like I knew the place, like I had taken its measure, but I now realized that nothing could have prepared me for how small I would feel in this valley of giants. It was shocking and a bit embarrassing how quickly I abandoned the idea of trying to climb El Capitan. Sure enough, I never got higher than a pitch off the ground during my first season in the valley.

I knew then that El Cap was something special. It was a cliff that would only reward those who put in their time, who worked hard for it, and who had the grit and determination to see it through no matter what it took to accomplish the summit. You simply had to earn it, and there were no shortcuts.

▲▲

It was early October, prime climbing season in Yosemite. Thermal updrafts wafted up El Capitan as swifts ripped through the air like tiny kamikaze dive-bombers. A group of local "dirtbag" climbers, who called themselves the Stone Monkeys, had been hard at work. The Monkeys had named themselves as a nod to their predecessors, the Stonemasters—the first well-known group of groundbreaking climbers that included Lynn Hill, who, after being the first person to free climb the Nose of El Capitan, upon topping out, simply said, "It goes, boys." Her now-famous words rival even George Mallory's "because it's there" quip about why he wanted to climb Mount Everest. The Stonemasters' unofficial leader at the time was none other than free soloist John Bachar. This next generation of Stone Monkeys broke new ground on the valley walls, establishing some of the world's most important long free climbs, such as Freerider, El Corazon, and Quantum Mechanic. They also took seriously their responsibility to carry on the rebellious antics the Stonemasters had enshrined into valley climbing lore.

When the Monkeys weren't practicing their craft on the valley's towering cathedrals, they were generally making a nuisance of themselves, loitering around a slackline (a tightrope of nylon webbing strung between two trees), staging bicycle demolition derbies in parking lots, making a ruckus in Camp 4 with all-night parties, and scouring tourist picnic tables in search of unfinished meals they could scavenge. At night, the Monkeys retreated to their various illegal bivouacs, where they hid from the park rangers. Despite the Stone Monkeys often mocking the politics of the park and dodging the rules that potentially limited their ease of access, they never failed to respect their obligations to the land itself. It was, after all, their playground, and there was nothing they wouldn't have done to protect it.

Lynn Hill. In 1993, she free climbed the Nose of El Capitan, a feat that many had deemed impossible. Afterward, she famously quipped, "It goes, boys."

The cliffs were their respite, their companions, even sometimes their nemeses, and they cared for these walls and valleys as anyone would their own home.

Cedar Wright, aka "Mr. Magoo," inhaled deeply, tilted back his head, and barked, "Oughh, ougghh." His guttural cry, which was meant to mimic a monkey but was closer to the sound made by an old dog with worn-out vocal chords, floated up the orange shield of rock that loomed above him. Someone was up there rappelling down the wall, and if it were a fellow Stone Monkey, he'd return the call. But whoever it was didn't reply.

"Holy shit, it's that Honnold kid," Cedar called to his partner, Nick Martino, when Alex came into view. Nick was fifty feet to the side of where Cedar was hanging at the belay for pitch twenty-four of Freerider. It was the pair's third day on the wall, and they were hoping to top out that evening. Neither of them knew Alex, but they certainly knew of him. For the past two weeks, the Monkeys had been all atwitter, as if a cobra had just slid into their nest, because some kid had come out of nowhere and free soloed two of the burliest routes in Yosemite—Astroman and Rostrum—back-to-back in the same day. Only one other person had ever done this—Peter Croft, twenty years before, in 1987.

Croft's feat had stunned the climbing world and shifted the paradigm of what people thought was possible. By 2007, Croft was a revered fixture in Yosemite, universally held in high esteem. He was quiet, reserved even, but had an easy, winning smile and was always friendly to anyone who came to talk to him.

He went about his business with little fanfare, a rarity for someone in his league. Unlike most other sports, climbing has no arena; there are no grand-stands at the base of the cliff. Nor is there a scoreboard or official results. If a climber wants his exploits known, he or his partner often just has to tell someone. Climbers call it "spraying," and for really good climbers—the ones with sponsorships and endorsement contracts—it's generally seen as a necessary part of the job.

No one denied that Croft was a genuinely humble man, and since he never cared to chase huge endorsement deals or sponsorships, he funded a simple lifestyle by working as a guide. He lived in a small house with his wife, drove a beater hatchback, and climbed every day.

Word might never have gotten out about Croft's Astroman-Rostrum linkup if it weren't for a chance encounter Croft had with another legend-ary climber, John Bachar. According to Bachar's account, he ran into Croft at the deli. Croft's hands were covered in chalk, and he had the unmistak-able look in his eyes that said he'd just been to another planet and back. Bachar knew the feeling, knew Croft had just done something big. He asked Croft what he had been up to. Croft dodged the question by taking a big bite of his sandwich. But Bachar wasn't going to let him off the hook until he'd spilled it, which Croft eventually did, sheepishly.

Bachar was floored when he figured it out. The thousand-foot Astroman represented the next level in free soloing. It was a climb that called for every trick in a Yosemite climber's bag, from thin, delicate face climbing to off-width cracks, like the infamous Harding Slot. Bachar had made the route's first free ascent in 1975, which meant he climbed it using only a rope for protection in case he fell. Before Bachar's free ascent, the route had only ever been climbed by those with fixed ropes and devices to help them ascend. Never in his wildest dreams did he imagine free soloing it.

Now the first person to repeat Croft's masterpiece, and only the third to free solo Astroman, was a dorky kid from Sacramento that no one had heard of.

The word circulating among the Monkeys was that Alex had only been climbing outdoors for three years. It wasn't unusual for a gym rat to make the transition to real rock and start pulling down big numbers at crags where the movement is similar to indoor climbing. Gym climbing had been exploding in popularity. With tens of thousands of young kids getting into the sport, it was inevitable that the overall level of climbing would rise accordingly. In the 1990s, there were only a handful of people capable of climbing the rarefied grade of 5.14. Ten years later, you could go to the local gym in any big city and probably find young kids climbing that hard. But no one had just shown up in Yosemite Valley and almost immediately mastered the vast repertoire of crack climbing techniques needed to do a route like Astroman, let alone free solo it.

The Monkeys had seen the kid around, and a few had spoken to him and climbed with him. But he was standoffish, which rubbed some people the wrong way. Rumor also had it that he drove his white Ford E-150 down Highway 140 every night to a pullout just outside the park boundary. The Monkeys took pride in their outlaw status, sleeping illegally under boulders, on ledges at the base of El Capitan, or in their vehicles in unoccupied campsites. But this Honnold kid actually followed the rules.

James "Peaches" Lucas was one of the few Stone Monkeys who could call Alex a friend in 2007. They had met the year before in Squamish and had climbed together a bit. "He was kind of an outlier," says James, because

Alex didn't care about being cool or about hanging out with the "in" crowd.

James was the one who reported Alex's Astroman-Rostrum free solo linkup on SuperTopo.com, an internet forum that was like Facebook for Yosemite climbers. The post didn't appear until six days after the event. In the interim, Alex had kept it under his hat.

> Last week, (Wednesday I think—which ever day NPS did the big controlled burn in the Valley) Alex Honold [*sic*] free soloed Astroman. Honold [*sic*] climbed the route doing the boulder problem pitch as well as the 11b variation higher. Later in the day he soloed the Regular North Face of the Rostrum using the unprotected 5.10 variation at the second pitch (there was a party on the 11a) Honold [*sic*] has also onsight free-soloed Pipeline (A Squamish Offwidth testpiece), the Lighning [*sic*] Bolt Cracks on the North Six Shooter, and soloed Chud a 13a at Rifle. Just wanted to send some props out to Alex. He's pretty modest so I figured I'd spray for him. Good job man.

"It was kind of a surprise to a lot of people that you could come to the valley and not hang out and be social and just rock climb and treat it as a serious sport," says James. "When you do that, and you're not spending all this time spraying, you get a lot more done. He's a really good example of someone who followed the textbook of what to do if you want to get good at climbing."

CHAPTER NINE
Moonlight Buttress

A post on SuperTopo titled "Alex Honnold Free Solos Moonlight Buttress" was posted April 4, 2008, a little less than seven months after Alex's Yosemite soloing binge. Everyone thought it was an April Fools' Day joke. Moonlight Buttress was not the kind of route that anyone would ever free solo. It's a 1,200-foot monolith in southwest Utah's Zion National Park capped with a vertical headwall whose only weakness is a finger-width crack that cleaves the orange sandstone like an expansion joint in the wall of a parking garage. In 2008, it was still impressive when someone climbed the route roped up without falling. It was ludicrous to think of someone topping it without a rope.

At first, neither *Climbing*, *Rock and Ice*, nor *Alpinist* magazines reported the climb on their websites, verifying in most people's minds that the post on SuperTopo had been a hoax. Then, on April 8, all three published stories confirming the free solo with firsthand accounts from Alex. Among other things, Alex said he didn't know that he'd done it on April 1. Because he lived in his van and climbed every day, one day often blurred into the next, and he almost never knew the day of the week, let alone the date.

As impressive as they were, one could understand climbing Astro-man and Rostrum without a rope, because it had been done before. Both are rated 5.11c, and Alex's best climb to date was 5.14b. But the Moonlight

Buttress is rated 5.12d, which (in the strange risk calculus climbers employ) trims the cushion, the margin for error, down by a grade and a half. Alex had just changed the game and annihilated everyone's idea of what a ropeless rock climber could do.

He'd done so by meticulous preparation and planning. Alex had spent two days practicing the route on a solo top rope, hiking to the top and fixing ropes all the way down. Each day he climbed the route top to bottom two times, taking a lunch break in between. There were a couple sections that he wanted to make sure he had fully dialed in. One was a face climbing move on pitch five where you surmount a feature called the Rocker Blocker. It's a five-by-three-foot loose block that teeters a few inches when you climb over it. Above the block is a long reach past a blank section to a secure hold shaped like an elephant ear. When Alex did the move, he looked down to see if he'd land on the Rocker Blocker if he slipped when he was free soloing. Nope. The key hold was just a smidge too far to the right. If he fell, he might bounce off the side of the Rocker Blocker, but there was no way it would stop him from falling to the ground.

He had planned to rest for one day and then go for it, but it rained, and you can't climb on sandstone when it's wet because the holds absorb water and become very fragile.

So he sat in his van in a movie theater parking lot by himself, running through the climb in his mind for hours on end. He thought about the individual moves, the sequences, how he would use his feet above the Rocker Blocker—and how glorious it was going to feel to hang up there on Moonlight Buttress with nothing but the tips of his fingers between him and eternity. But he also thought about how things could go wrong and what it would feel like if he slipped. Rather than hide from this reality, he explored it, right down to picturing how it would feel to hit the ground at terminal velocity. In his mind's eye, he hovered above his crumpled, bloody body. It was all part of his preparation. He wanted to think about it now, thoroughly, so he didn't have to when he was up on the wall. Get it out of his system, so to speak. This way there wouldn't be any surprises. People walked in and out of the movie theater, but no one noticed Alex sitting in his van. Later, he realized that he had been so lost in his head that he couldn't remember if he had gone to a movie or not.

The night of March 31, he cooked himself mac and cheese on his Coleman double burner, and afterward he watched a police drama called *The Shield* on his laptop. At eight p.m. he went to sleep.

The next morning, he drove into the park early. Like Yosemite, the six-mile-long Zion Canyon is lined with some of the biggest cliffs in the country, including the Court of the Patriarchs—Abraham, Isaac, and Jacob—a cluster of three soaring towers of vermillion sandstone that Alex admired as he drove past. A mile from the end of the canyon, where it dead-ends at the famous slot called the Narrows, Alex pulled into a turnout below the north face of Angels Landing. On the other side of the Virgin River, Moonlight Buttress glowed in the morning sun. Alex hadn't seen a soul or told anyone what he intended to do. He waded barefoot through the ice-cold, emerald-colored river, holding his rock shoes in his hand, then scampered up the trail to the base of the buttress. The plan had been to wait until the route went into the shade at ten a.m., but he was so amped he couldn't hold himself back. He took off all the layers he had on until he got to his cotton T-shirt, then hit play on his iPod. As a speed metal band called

Alex Honnold high on the Moonlight Buttress in Zion National Park during the re-creation of his historic ropeless ascent.

Bad Religion began to pump through the headphones, he grabbed the first hold and pulled down.

The average climbing party takes three days to climb Moonlight Buttress. They sleep in small tents called portaledges suspended off the side of the cliff by carabiners and webbing. These tents typically have a small platform where the climbers eat, sleep, and rest. It's a cramped living space, to say the least, and unlike being in a tent at a campground, you are hanging high up from the base of the cliff. There's no opportunity to take an evening walk or take a break from your climbing partners for a few minutes. Normally, a climber spends two nights on Moonlight Buttress, hauling bags full of provisions and aid-climbing most of the route, which means that they pull themselves up using gear they place in the cracks, rather than climb the rock itself with their hands and feet. Alex, wearing nothing but the shirt on his back and a pair of rock shoes and a chalk bag, topped out eighty-three minutes after he had set off from the base—with a few songs left on his playlist. Strangely, he felt more pride in breaking the speed record than in being the first person to climb the route without a rope.

On the descent down the back, Alex joined a popular trail leading to the summit of Angels Landing, where he passed dozens of tourists. His climbing shoes, being too tight for hiking, hung on his waist from the same belt of thin nylon webbing holding his chalk bag. A few people felt the need to let Alex know how foolish he was for hiking barefoot. Alex smiled and chuckled to himself. An hour later he was on the road, driving back to his mom's house in Sacramento.

CHAPTER TEN
The First Free Solo Film

In the days following the climb, Alex was bombarded with emails and calls from photographers and filmmakers who wanted to shoot him on the route. He told them all the same thing: "Thanks but no thanks." All the mileage he had put in on Moonlight had caused the tendonitis in his elbow to flare up, and he just wanted to hang out at his mom's house, eat cookie dough, and keep binge-watching *The Shield*.

Months later, though, Alex had a change of heart. Perhaps, he reasoned, it made sense to go back and re-create the climb. People were calling it the boldest free solo in history, and it was a shame that he had no record of it. His friend Celin Serbo, a photographer from Boulder, Colorado, had expressed interest, and Alex had also been talking with another climber turned filmmaker named Peter Mortimer. Alex called them both and told them that he'd changed his mind.

The night before the re-creation, they went out for pizza in Springdale, the gateway to Zion National Park. As they sat around hashing out the logistics for the shoot, Peter shivered, like he had just seen a ghost. The image of the wide-eyed kid sitting across from him free-falling down the side of Moonlight Buttress flashed across his mind. Peter was not only an award-winning filmmaker but also a skilled climber, and he'd climbed the route that Alex was attempting before. He knew exactly how hard and tenuous Moonlight Buttress was. The plan had sounded great back in Boulder, but now that it was happening, he wasn't so sure.

After dinner, Alex headed for his van, and Peter, his assistant, Jim Aikman, and Celin went to their hotel.

"Guys," said Peter a little later that evening, sitting on the edge of the bed. "I'm having second thoughts about what we're doing here."

"Me too," said Celin.

They talked it over. Nothing had happened yet.

No one slept well that night. Peter tossed and turned as his mind worked through all the various layers of what it would mean if Alex fell. He knew that it would impact his career and that people would blame him for encouraging—if not subtly pressuring—Alex to do the climb again for the cameras. But more than that, he simply couldn't bear the thought of Alex dying. "I didn't know him that well," says Peter, "but I liked him and felt close to him. He was one of the most refreshing people I'd ever met because he was so real and genuine. There was no pretense. You knew you were talking to the real Alex." The central question swirling in his mind was whether or not Alex was doing this for the right reasons. They were in Zion to re-create one of the most amazing climbs in history. How exactly could this be seen as anything other than self-aggrandizement? *What is my responsibility here?* wondered Peter.

"Hey, dudes, what's up?" said Alex casually, in his deep baritone voice, when they met up for breakfast the next morning. The whole scene felt surreal to Peter, but he played along, projecting a confidence he didn't feel.

"Cool, man, yeah, let's do it," said Peter.

Two hours later, Alex was standing on a ledge the width of a staircase tread, eight hundred feet off the deck. Celin and Peter hung nearby, framing up their respective shots. They had all hiked up the back of Moonlight Buttress and rappelled off the top. Alex never intended to repeat the entire free solo for the cameras. Instead, he would just do the final three pitches of the route, which were the most visually striking and dramatic moves. He slipped off his harness, clipped it to the end of the rope, and called up to Celin that he could pull it up out of the shot. It was eight a.m., and the temperature was still only in the low fifties, but a light breeze made it feel colder. Alex wore long gray pants and a red T-shirt with a light blue polypropylene long-sleeved shirt underneath. His only accoutrement, apart from the rock shoes on his feet, was a purple chalk bag held to his waist with a piece of nylon webbing. A gray-handled toothbrush, for brushing excess chalk off handholds, was slotted in an elastic sleeve on the side of the bag.

Staring down the wall, the group could see three aid-climbing parties below. Two were starting up from the base, and one had spent the night in a portaledge a few pitches above the ground. Peter recalls Alex looking down at the "gumbies" and saying something like, "This is [expletive], all this posing. I should just solo the whole route again. Freak all those people out. Show them what real climbing is all about."

But the show, such as they had construed it, was set to begin, so Alex jammed his fingers into the perfect crack splitting the headwall above him and stepped off the ledge. The walls on either side of the crack were sandy and smooth, almost without imperfection. The only possible purchase was in the crack itself. Alex buried his fingers into it and twisted his arm and wrist to lock them in place. He tucked the tips of his toes in the crack as well. As he reached for the next fingerlock, his continued existence hung from the digits of one hand. On the tighter jams, the ones where the crack pinched down to half an inch, he could only get the tips of his index and middle fingers into the crack. But most of the time he was able to sink all four fingers to the hilt. When the jams were shaped like peapods, tapering down into tight constrictions, he would slide his fingers into the crack with his thumb on top. The meat of these jams rested on his pinky. He loved these "pinky locks" because they didn't require the same arm torque as thumb-down jams, and he could extend to his full wingspan between moves.

Staring through the viewfinder on his camera, Peter gasped at the footage he was capturing. What Alex was doing seemed almost inhuman. On a visceral level, it seemed to violate some unspecified law of nature. Peter felt sick.

As if in answer, Alex looked up the wall toward the two cameramen as he clung to the tiny fissure in the vertical wall of stone.

"Is this even cool?" he asked. "Do you want me to breathe hard and make it look like I'm scared or I'm trying?"

CHAPTER ELEVEN
Half Dome

In September of 2008, about five months after his free solo of Moonlight Buttress, Alex found himself alone and unroped near the top of the northwest face of Half Dome—and things were not going according to plan. One moment he was a hero, a demigod, feeling confident about his abilities. Then, in an instant, he felt as though he was barely clinging to the side of a cliff that he had vastly underestimated. As his armor dissolved like an apparition, it felt like waking up from a pleasant dream into a nightmare. Alex had climbed himself into the ultimate dead end nearly two thousand feet up the side of one of the most famous cliffs in the world, and no one but himself could get him out of it.

He knew what he needed to do, because he had climbed the route a few days earlier with a rope, but he hadn't meticulously rehearsed this climb. That kind of precision and discipline would come later in his career. A few days earlier, this move felt scary-hard and was the one crux on the whole route that he hadn't felt good about. But he told himself that he must have screwed up the sequence and he'd just find an easier way to execute the move when he got up there without a rope. The day before, he had called his friend Chris Weidner, who had become his confidant, and told him what he was planning to do.

"What?" said Chris. "Are you crazy? You need to rehearse the [heck] out of it before you try to solo it."

"I've thought about that," said Alex. "And I've decided I want to keep it exciting." When Alex completed Moonlight Buttress five months earlier, he'd done an extensive amount of rehearsal before the free solo. As a result, the climb had felt "gimmicky." So he decided he'd figure this one out when he got there.

But now that he was facing down the move, he realized his lack of preparation was a mistake. This was simply and unavoidably a horribly insecure move, and without a rope to practice the different options to get past it, he essentially had no choice but to do it the way he had a few days before, because at least he knew that sequence was doable. It meant pasting his right foot onto a tiny ripple and rocking his weight onto it while crimping two tiny creases with his fingers. If the foot didn't slip, he could then reach through to a good hold above. But if the foot did slip? Well, that outcome was unthinkable.

The spot he was stuck in was no picnic either. He wasn't on a ledge resting while he contemplated how to free himself from this predicament. The creases he gripped with his fingers were too thin to hold himself up with just his hands. His feet were perched on two small edges in the rock. Most of his weight was on his toes, and his feet and calves were beginning to burn. Footholds like these have a tendency to degrade the longer you stand on them. The friction of the boot rubber against the rock creates heat, which causes the shoe to slowly ooze off the hold. It feels like falling off the mountain in slow motion.

He shifted his weight from one foot to the other while doing the same with his hands. His hands were wet with sweat, so he kept reaching back to dip his fingers into his chalk bag. Alex needed to calm down, so he tried to take some deep breaths. *You've got this*, he told himself. But it didn't work. He knew he didn't have it; he was teetering on the edge of control. Every second that he didn't execute the move gave way to further muscle fatigue and more space in his mind for doubt. Half a dozen times, he threw his right foot onto the offending hold. *Do it, do it, do it*, he willed himself, but something wouldn't let him.

If he truly had no choice, he might already have dispensed with the move, whatever the outcome. But there was another option: right in front of his face a shiny bolt protruded from the rock, and clipped to that bolt was a fat oval carabiner. It hung on the wall inches from his right hand. He could grab it, pull himself up, and reach past this horrible move. A body length above him the difficulty eased way off. If he used the carabiner, he could be on the summit in seconds.

He could hear the chatter of tourists up there. It was a warm late-summer afternoon. A few hundred feet above him, dozens of people were taking photos, hugging, laughing, loving life. He looked up to see if any of them were watching him. It's a common thing for tourists to get on their stomachs and inch out onto a block called the Diving Board that overhangs the vertical northwest face. BASE jumpers use it as their launchpad. Thankfully, no one was watching him.

Just grab the carabiner, a voice inside his head whispered. *It's not worth it. Don't throw your life away for one dumb rock climb.* But another voice, equally powerful, said, *Wait, don't give up yet. You're one move away from the greatest free solo in history. Do you really want to throw away all the climbing you've done to get to this point?* And at that moment, Alex realized that if he didn't complete this free solo, right now, it was likely that no one ever would.

But some unconscious force in his mind simply wouldn't permit him to rock his weight onto his right foot. Each time he lifted it up and placed it on the subtle protrusion, he froze. He was about to give in and grab the carabiner when he had an idea. By shifting the load-bearing onto his middle and ring fingers, he would be able to extend his index finger and lay the first pad on the bottom lip of the carabiner. He touched it *ever* so gently, making sure not to weight it even an ounce. This would be his compromise. He'd pull the move like this, and if the foot slipped, he'd hook his finger through the carabiner and hold on for dear life. It offered a slim possibility of survival should he blow it. He threw the right foot onto the ripple and, with all his weight still on the toes of his left foot, inhaled deeply.

Alex suddenly felt confident and more relaxed. He weighted the right toe and bore down as hard as he could on his fingertips, still making sure not to put weight on the carabiner. The foot held, and he snatched for an incut edge with his left hand. Done. He charged up the final crack leading to the summit and, as he topped out, passed about twenty people sitting on the edge of the cliff. He half expected—hoped—that someone would yell, "Hey, everybody, check it out—this madman just free soloed the northwest face of Half Dome." But no one said a word. He might as well have been invisible.

Shirtless, panting, he looked at his chalk-covered hands and wrists and the veins bulging from his forearms. He looked around again. It was a beautiful sunny day. A hundred tourists were spread out across the summit of the dome, reveling in the views of the surrounding Sierra Nevada Mountains and congratulating themselves on the strenuous ten-mile hike to the summit of such a remarkable geologic formation. No one noticed him. Not one single person. Why would they? The last thing anyone would have been looking for was the equivalent of Spider-Man coming up the underside of the cliff, especially on his own with no support team to draw attention to him.

Alex took off his shoes, strung them through the belt of his chalk bag, and headed off for the cables leading down the slabs on the east side of the dome. And then, finally, someone addressed him.

"Oh my god," called out the tourist. Alex looked up hopefully. "You're hiking barefoot. You're so tough."

It had been a conscious decision for Alex to climb Half Dome without major rehearsal beforehand—it was part of his style. However, lessons learned from this endeavor would serve him well over the next nine years in his quest for the free solo of El Cap.

PART TWO

THE PROFESSIONAL WORLD

CHAPTER TWELVE
Borneo

In 2009, I took Alex on his first expedition to climb a remote cliff in Borneo. The expedition began in Kota Kinabalu (or KK), a coastal city partly surrounded by the rain forest. KK is home to nearly 550,000 people and ringed with tropical beaches. It reminded me of Honolulu. What I didn't know is that Borneo, the world's third-largest island, is divided between three different countries. Three-quarters of the island is Indonesian territory, while the northern portion is mostly part of Malaysia, except for a 2,200-square-mile enclave on the north coast owned by the tiny nation of Brunei.

The genesis of this trip, like many of my expeditions, is kind of interesting. In November 1999, I was climbing in northern Cameroon, and one night I found myself in a dusty camp below a volcanic spire. My friend Greg Child and I were sitting around a campfire listening to some tall tales being spun by our South African climbing partners, Edmund February and Andy DeKlerk. They talked of a mysterious jungle canyon lined with titanic cliffs that might be as tall as ten thousand vertical feet. I was in awe and nearly jumped out of my skin at the thought of climbing something of that magnitude.

"Pleeeease, just tell me where it is," I begged.

"Yeah, well, the thing is, we can't tell you, because we're thinking about climbing it ourselves," said Ed.

"You're the last guy we'd tell," said Andy. They were worried, of course, that I'd beat them to it.

I had mostly forgotten about that conversation when, many years later, I came across a book called *Descent into Chaos*. The book told the story of how a British Army expedition unsuccessfully attempted the first descent of Low's Gully, the world's deepest slot canyon, located on the north side of Mount Kinabalu in Borneo. One look at the cover—an image of a jungle gully flanked with towering cliffs—and I knew I had found the secret climbing paradise that I'd first heard of back in Cameroon.

I convinced the North Face to sponsor an expedition to Borneo, and Jimmy Chin, Conrad Anker, Renan Ozturk, Kevin Thaw, and the new young climbing sensation Alex Honnold joined me. It was Conrad's idea to invite Alex; he thought he could be our "secret weapon," a fearless young buck to send out on the sharp end when the older climbers were tapped out and a tough pitch needed to be fired. By "older climbers," of course, he was referring to the rest of us, who, despite all still climbing hard, were on average twenty years Alex's senior.

I arrived at our hotel in Borneo in the middle of the night after two long days of shuffling across twelve time zones. I was too frazzled to sleep, so I fell into a chair and tried to relax. When I heard a knock at the door, I got up to find Alex Honnold standing in the hallway. I invited him in, and he took a seat on the bed. It was the first time I'd sat face-to-face and talked with the guy, and I was immediately captivated by his eyes, which were deer-in-the-headlights huge.

"Vodka?" I offered, holding up the bottle.

"I don't drink," he said. "Never have. I don't smoke or use caffeine either."

"What did you bring to read?" I asked. I'd learned long ago that you could never have too much reading material on a climbing trip.

"I brought twelve books," he replied.

"Twelve?"

"Yeah, and I'm glad I did because I've already read two." Alex rattled off some titles that included *The Brothers Karamazov* by Fyodor Dostoyevsky and several philosophical treatises on atheism.

We talked a bit about Half Dome. It had only been about six months since the free solo, and people were calling it the boldest rock climb in the history of the sport. Alex told me the story, explaining how he "lost his armor" on that slabby face on pitch twenty-one. "I should have spent more time preparing the route," he said.

"So, what about El Cap?" I asked. In the two years since he had turned the global climbing scene on its head, he had already established himself as the best free soloist in history. And everyone knew that a free solo of El Capitan was the holy grail of rock climbing. Whoever did it would go down in history as the greatest climber ever. Dean Potter, the notorious free soloist and BASE jumper, had been eyeing it. No disrespect to the Dark Wizard (Dean's nickname in the climbing community), but everyone knew it was beyond him. But this kid sitting across from me was operating in a whole new realm. It still seemed far-fetched, and I doubted it would actually happen, but every new generation of climbers pushes the boundaries beyond what the previous one thought possible. It was an obvious question to ask, though somewhat impertinent. Climbers tend to be coy about their grandest ambitions and likewise respect one another's reticence. But Alex had an air of frank openness that made me think he

Dean Potter slacklining at Taft Point, with El Capitan visible in the background.

wouldn't mind me asking. And honestly, I was extremely curious to find out whether he would seriously consider it or not.

"I do think about it," said Alex, "but right now it's way too scary. Maybe someday, though. We'll see." With that, he stood up, arched his back, and started toward the door.

"Well, it was good to finally meet you," he said as he stepped out of the room.

"Actually, we've already met," I replied. Alex looked at me inquisitively, tilting his head to the side, then shrugged and walked away.

That meeting had only been a few weeks earlier at a rock climbing festival in the desert outside of Las Vegas. It was dark and noisy, and the only thing I remember from the encounter, apart from its brevity, was the handshake. As Alex's mitt closed around mine, I felt like a little kid shaking hands with a giant. It was a peculiar sensation, because I'm taller and heftier than he is, and he didn't have a commanding presence otherwise. He stood hunched forward, shoulders drooped, dark eyes hidden under his hoodie like some shadowy character from a Star Wars movie.

I had always put climbers in one of two categories: those who'd had the wake-up call, and those who hadn't. Until a climber has experienced a serious accident, it's easy to feel invincible and to fall into the trap of thinking that bad things just don't happen to you. Someone like Conrad, who had lost several of his best friends to climbing accidents and nearly died himself in an avalanche in Tibet—he certainly had his eyes wide open. But what about Alex? His eyes appeared to be wide open, but were they really? Did he recognize how close he was to the edge?

CHAPTER THIRTEEN
Getting Prepped in Borneo

The trail to the summit of Mount Kinabalu was muddy and narrow as it wound its way below waterfalls and along spiny ridges bordered with wind-stunted trees. Pitcher plants of every possible size and color littered the ground. Birds darted from tree to tree. Colorful butterflies floated in the air all around us. The slopes of Mount Kinabalu host ecosystems of dazzling diversity. Botanists are still finding new species every year within the six unique ecological zones that lie along the mountain's flank. The latest tally puts the total number of plant species on Kinabalu at approximately six thousand, which is more than Europe and North America combined. This number includes eight hundred species of orchids, six hundred species of ferns, and twenty-seven different types of rhododendrons.

As we climbed higher, the wind picked up and we entered a cloud forest where everything was coated in electric-green moss that grew up the trunks of the trees and hung beard-like from the branches. Orchids grew from niches in dead logs and in the crotches of trees. I kept sniffing for the park's most famous plant—*Rafflesia arnoldii*, aka the "stinking corpse lily." It's the world's largest flower, and its petals can grow to more than three feet in diameter. Its smell, as one might guess, is said to be nauseating, but I never managed to get a whiff of it.

From left to right: Conrad Anker, Jimmy Chin, and Alex Honnold on the approach to Low's Gully on Mount Kinabalu in Borneo.

When Jimmy and I finally crested a ridge at sunset, we found Conrad and Alex sitting next to a giant pile of duffel bags. It was raining, the wind was gusting, and it would be dark in a few minutes. There was nothing even vaguely resembling flat ground anywhere.

"Mind if I bivy with you?" asked Alex, looking mildly concerned.

"Of course. Check and see if you can find any good spots for the tent down the ridge. I'm going to check over here." Half an hour later, neither of us had found anything, so we just pitched the tent next to the pile of bags. The spot was a jumbled pile of boulders, which was far from ideal but no worse than anywhere else in the vicinity. After guying out the tent, we unzipped it and looked inside. I burst out laughing. Alex didn't laugh, but he did smile when he saw the jagged spine of rock running down the middle of the tent floor. "We'll find a better spot in the morning," I said, crawling in. I went to work leveling my side by filling the nooks and crannies with rolled up duffel bags, books, and anything else I could find. With the foundation laid, I inflated my Therm-a-Rest pad and laid it over the mess. Pumped nice and stiff, it covered the chaos underneath well enough. Next, I reached into the bottom of my duffel and pulled out the pillow from my bed at home, which was warm and dry inside a black Hefty trash bag. I propped the pillow against the back wall and laid back while emitting an exaggeratedly loud sigh of contentment. Alex, who was still sitting in the door of the tent, gave me a bemused look. "You brought your pillow?" he said.

"Of course," I replied, relishing the moment. "I always do. Didn't you?" Alex didn't answer. He wasn't willing to accept that I had something to offer him from my years of experience, and that was okay for now. He was going to tough it out in an uncomfortable sleeping situation just so he didn't need to address his own inexperience. Sleeping on the ground was one thing, and it's even understandable that one might think it silly to take up valuable real estate in your pack with a bulky pillow, but a good night's sleep is worth a lot when you're soon to be living on the side of a cliff. Alex's character—not to mention his trust in me, Jimmy, and Conrad—was about to be truly tested.

CHAPTER FOURTEEN
Mr. Safety and the Secret Weapon

In the morning, Conrad and I took on the mission of finding a way down into the gully, while the rest of the team stayed behind to work on our base camp. The biggest drawback to the camp wasn't its precariousness; it was the lack of water. The only source I could find was a soupy puddle skimmed with a layer of black gunk and a giant white dead bug floating inside it. The jungle rats that were trying to infiltrate our food stash were another unwelcome discovery.

According to my research there were two routes down into the gully: the path taken by the British Army back in 1994 through a place called Lone Tree and an alternate route established by a Spanish team back in 2000, which is the one we'd follow. We planned to rappel into Low's Gully and then climb a giant wall back out the other side to a summit called the Donkey Ears. In 2004, a British team followed the Spaniards' lead, and while I was bummed that we wouldn't be the first, I was also encouraged to know that reputable climbers had deemed the canyon a worthy objective.

The next morning, after rappelling about two thousand feet into an algae-covered riverbed, Alex and I stood at the base of the wall we had come to climb.

"Where's your helmet?" I asked.

"Uhhh, I don't have one," he replied sheepishly.

"What do you mean? You forgot it back in camp?" Before I finished my question, I knew the answer.

"Uhhh, no. I mean I didn't bring one on the trip."

"Intentionally?"

"Sort of. I don't actually own a helmet."

The conversation could have been comical if we had been any place on earth other than where we were. Imposing walls of crumbly granite hung above us in every direction. The gully was about thirty feet across, and every time it rained there would be debris-ridden flash floods running through its polished walls. It was not the kind of place you ventured without a helmet.

Below us, the gully dropped out of sight into a mist-filled cauldron. If we were canyoneers, we could have kept rappelling into the abyss. Six miles farther down the canyon and ten thousand feet below, the gully would eventually spill us into the South China Sea. At the time, only three parties had ever successfully negotiated the canyon, one of which had barely survived.

We intended to pioneer our own route up this cliff, but the flash floods made the bottom few hundred feet of the wall porcelain smooth, and it made no sense to drill bolts alongside the ones that were already in place. We decided to follow a line of bolts the Spanish had drilled into the wall until we found a good spot to branch off into uncharted territory.

But Alex was doing it all wrong. Instead of walking up his etriers (nylon ladders) and hanging in his harness between moves, he was pulling himself upward using only his arms. By this point I had climbed at least fifty big walls, and I had never seen anyone do it this way.

"Hey, there's an easier way to do that," I yelled up.

"I know," he called back. "I want to do it this way, so I can get more of a workout." I laughed, my cackle echoing in the cave-like chamber. It was ridiculous what he was doing, but wasn't that the whole point of climbing: to bend over backward and make life as difficult as possible?

On the second pitch, I was thirty feet above Alex's hanging belay when I noticed a detached flake blocking the path forward. I lightly tapped my knuckles on the block, like I was knocking on someone's front door. It sounded like a drum. All four sides were cracked, and I wondered what was holding it to the wall. "Just free climb around it," called Alex, when he saw that I had stalled out. But the rock was covered in lichen, and there were no good holds to pull on—other than the block itself. What I did next is the climbing equivalent of grabbing the handle on a skillet to see if it's hot. I slid a small camming device into the crack on the bottom of the flake and gave it a tug. As the cam lobes flexed outward, whatever flimsy bond that was adhering the block to the wall came unglued. A horrible grinding noise filled the air. A chunk the size and shape of a cinder block slammed into my chest, tearing through three layers of clothing and taking a bite out of my pectoral muscle before continuing its flight downward.

"ROCK!" I screamed as I watched it spin through the air, making a sound like a swooshing samurai sword. Alex leaned to the side nonchalantly as the rock sailed past about a body length away. A few seconds later, it cratered into the gully below, sending a shock wave up the wall and echoing across

Easy Valley. My body shook with adrenaline. Blood oozed from the gash in my chest. I leaned the rim of my helmet against the wall and gazed between my legs at my helmetless partner. We shared a silent look that said, *See, man, maybe a helmet isn't such a bad idea.*

Two days later, Alex and I rappelled back into the gully. This time, we weren't going back to base camp at the end of the day. Our task was to push the route forward while the rest of the team followed behind hauling up the gear we'd need to spend the next week living on the cliff. It was exciting to think that somewhere up on the wall, I didn't know where, we would bivouac in portaledges that night. We had reached the point where it was time to branch off the Spanish route, and my mind was filled with that feeling of giddy anticipation that comes with going off the map, outside the known world.

To my secret delight, Alex had shown up that day wearing a light blue helmet. He had quietly borrowed it from Ozturk, who was staying behind to film the ascent. He was going to shoot long shots of us working our way up the wall.

By late morning, I found myself in a precarious position. I was hanging from a camming device wedged between two plates of rock that moved when I shifted my weight. Sand and pebbles sifted out from beneath the plates—never a good sign. I was filled with uncertainty and dread as I began to realize that the path I'd chosen was a minefield. I tapped the rocks to the side and above me with my hammer, like playing a xylophone. Each piece had its own unique tone, but I couldn't find the sharp metallic ring of solid rock anywhere. It was like I was playing a game of Jenga, but with bigger consequences. If I chose poorly, as I had done on the second pitch, and accidentally dislodged the wrong piece of stone, it was possible I could unload a dump truck's worth of loose rock onto myself, Alex, and everyone else down below.

"Go for it," Alex yelled impatiently from his perch twenty feet below me. "It's not dangerous if you tread lightly." He was right. This type of climbing, what we call "choss," had once been my specialty. Over the years, I'd free climbed some notoriously sketchy routes, like Stratosfear in Colorado's Black Canyon, the east face of Mount Babel in the Canadian Rockies, and most of a new route on Mount Dickey in Alaska. But you need confidence, and a lot of it, to free climb on loose rock, and at this moment, I couldn't muster any.

When I called for the bolt kit, Alex didn't hide his disgust. "Seriously?" he said. "You're going to drill?" When I affirmed that indeed was my plan, he said I was being "super old-school," a thinly veiled way of telling me he thought I was a wimp. Drilling a bolt is the one way in which climbers permanently alter the landscape. Once that four-inch-deep hole is bored into the rock, it will be there forever. For this reason, many climbers, myself included, try to avoid using bolts, if at all possible. I had to weigh the question of whether I was violating climbing's unwritten ethical code against the chance that I would fall, pull out all my protection, and break my legs when I hit the ledge where Alex was holding my rope. Picturing myself crumpled and broken was all the convincing I needed.

An hour later, I pulled onto a sloping ledge three feet deep and fifteen feet long. I had only climbed about a third the length of a normal pitch, but this shelf offered the perfect location for our bivouac—and I was happy for an excuse to stop and build an anchor. The cracks I'd been following had petered out, and the next weakness was hundreds of feet away, at the end of a long section of overhanging gray rock that that didn't seem to have any weaknesses in which to place protection. If I were to continue, it would mean drilling a ladder of bolts up the wall. No one wanted to see that happen, least of all an impatient and pacing Alex Honnold waiting to be let out of his cage.

"Time for the secret weapon," I said to myself as I reeled in the rope for Alex, who was in a sour mood when he joined me on the ledge. "What the hell have you done to my cams?" he demanded. I had undone some rubber bands on the slings of his camming devices because I needed the carabiners to build my anchor. My pitch was short, but I'd been so scared that I'd managed to stick most of our rack into the mountain. I explained why I thought it didn't make sense to have the biners banded on to each camming device for multiday big wall climbs. "I think I know how to take care of my cams and biners," he spat.

"Why don't you clip in?" I asked. Alex was standing next to me on the ledge, and he wasn't connected to anything. I thought this was an unnecessary risk, and I told him so. But I had lost all credibility in his eyes, and he was done having "Mr. Safety"—the nickname he had given me somewhere along the way—mentor him. He stayed untethered.

I assumed Alex had always been a nitpicker, but his friend Chris Weidner later told me that Alex's attitude began to change in 2009. Chris first met Alex in 2006, before he was famous, and he says that in those early days, Alex was soft-spoken, thoughtful, and generous to a fault. When they climbed a route called Golden Gate on El Capitan in 2007, Alex practically dragged Chris up the wall. "He was a really, really supportive partner, even though, compared to him, I sucked." But over the next few years, as Alex's fame grew and he became a public figure, Chris says he also became more self-centered. "I don't know whether he was getting a little older and more comfortable in his skin or what," recounts Chris, "but he definitely changed a bit, and I wasn't too psyched about it." According to Chris, Alex couldn't understand why his friend wasn't as motivated or as strong as he was or why he didn't see things the same way he did. He was showing zero empathy and being selfish "in the way that a psychopath is selfish," says Chris.

"It was insane how obsessive and nitpicky he was: 'Why do you need to drink that cup of coffee? Why are you drinking that wine? Why do you put so much salt on your dinner?'" It got so bad that Chris stopped using salt because it was easier than battling Alex about it.

As Alex grumpily put the rubber bands back onto his cams, Jimmy joined us on the ledge. He grabbed the carabiner of hooks and went through them with Alex like they were keys on a key ring. There was the talon, the sky hook, the fish hook, the pointed Leeper, and the flat Leeper. We even had a custom hook I had shaped on my grinding wheel at home. I called it the Hawk, for its beak-like point and because I came up with the idea for it while listening to a classic rock station of the same name on El Capitan. Jimmy placed the hooks on variously shaped edges on the wall in front of us, explaining why he chose one over the other and showing Alex how to test if a placement was solid. He put the sky hook, which is shaped like a shepherd's crook, onto a chip the size of a silver dollar. When he weighted it, the metal dug behind the tiny flake and popped it off like a dead toenail. "Choose wisely," said Jimmy, chuckling as he gave me a knowing look.

Just a few months before, Jimmy had led a pitch like this at twenty thousand feet in the Indian Himalayas on Mount Meru. More than twenty different expeditions, which included some of the best alpinists in the world, had attempted the route previously, but no one had come close to success. Jimmy's masterful lead, which Conrad later named the House of Cards because of the rock's instability, proved to be the key to the route. But the team ran out of food and fuel and ended up turning back just a hundred meters shy of the summit. (This was their first attempt, and they'd return to finish the route in 2011.)

Alex set off, moving slowly upward, making long reaches between small holds I couldn't see. He kicked some of the footholds to test their integrity before stepping on them. *Good*, I thought, *he's showing some caution*. His route meandered right, then back left, then straight over a bulge to a small stance twenty-five feet above, where he was splayed out on the wall like a gecko. His rope whipsawed in the air, and I tried to calculate if the wall was steep enough that he would miss the ledge if he fell.

"That's far enough," called Jimmy. "Try to find a good hook placement and get a bolt in." Crimping an edge with his left hand, Alex reached down and pulled the hooks off the gear loop on the right side of his harness. He chose one and placed it on edge in front of his chest. He gave it a little downward tug, and, satisfied it was good, he clipped his harness to it with a short sling called a quick draw and slowly eased his weight onto it while still holding on with his fingers in case it popped off.

"Is it normal for the hook to flex?" he called down nervously as his life

Jimmy Chin on the wall in Borneo. Low's Gully, which drops ten thousand vertical feet over six miles, is visible below him.

hung from a quarter inch of chrome-moly steel balanced on a chip of rock the width of a matchbox.

"Perfectly normal," I yelled back. Then Alex drilled his first bolt. Moving up toward what looked like a ledge, he stretched the rope to its end, placing four more bolts along the way. When he called down off belay about two hours after he had set off, Jimmy and I looked at each other.

The kid had just on-sighted loose, overhanging 5.12 on a jungle wall in Borneo. And he made it look easy. I wasn't confident I could follow his lead, even with the rope overhead, so I seconded the pitch by clamping mechanical ascenders to the rope and ratcheting my way upward. When I got to the anchor, I looked up at Alex. His brown eyes were wide open, and the way he looked at me was entirely different than he ever had before. The grumpiness was gone, and in its place was a glow that came not just from his eyes and the huge grin that covered his face—it seemingly radiated from his entire being. I felt like I had just come in from the cold and was now standing next to a blazing fire. And I realized why Conrad had fallen under Alex's spell when they climbed El Niño together on El Capitan. Being near Alex when he was luminescent felt really good. "That was sick," said Alex. "I'm so stoked." We went for a high five, but I turned my hand sideways and clasped his giant fingers. He looked at me and smiled.

We reached the summit three days later. It was beautiful but anticlimactic, as they always seem to be. We work so hard and take so many risks on these climbs that I suppose it's inevitable that mountaintops hardly ever live up to the monumental billing we attach to them. The letdown is so common that some climbers have said that summits don't matter. It's a gallant idea, but if the summit doesn't matter, where exactly are we heading when we set off from the base?

Conrad was right when he told me that I would learn a lot from climbing with "the kid." Alex Honnold reminded me of the old climbing proverb: "There are old climbers and there are bold climbers, but there are no old bold climbers." He helped me to see, perhaps for the first time, how cautious I had become over the past few years. What I hadn't realized until Borneo was that if I kept reeling things in at the rate I was going, it was only a matter of time before I wouldn't have any desire to climb a first ascent like the one we'd just done.

After my dad had told me that I would be "worm food" when I died, I had been desperate to find something that could give meaning to my existence. Then I found climbing and, perhaps more importantly, the climbing community. Climbing became my passion, and the strength of that passion gave my life the orientation and purpose it had previously lacked. Climbing taught me what the fox meant when he told the Little Prince, "One sees clearly only with the heart. Anything essential is invisible to the eye."

CHAPTER FIFTEEN
Nonprofit

Thanks in part to a *60 Minutes* profile that aired in 2011, Alex was slowly becoming a household name in America, which was unusual for climbers. He starred in a commercial for Citibank, signed an endorsement deal with the North Face, and even considered climbing the world's tallest building— the 2,700-foot Burj Khalifa in Dubai—live on TV. That last one didn't end up happening, but Alex's name recognition skyrocketed.

Despite his increased fame, Alex continued to live in his van, and his annual expenses ran about $15,000 a year. He made a lot more money than he used to, but he was still living off a pittance. Financial advisers suggested that he invest his extra into the stock market, but Alex had something different in mind.

A year earlier, in the fall of 2010, Alex, myself, and a few others, including Jimmy Chin, teamed up for an expedition to Chad. We became the first technical climbers to explore a twenty-five-thousand-square-mile area called the Ennedi Plateau, which lies on the southern fringe of the Sahara Desert. We made first ascents of about twenty freestanding sandstone towers, but it wasn't the climbing that left an impression on Alex. The trip was Alex's first to the African continent, and in 2010, Chad was the fourth-poorest country in the world. Life expectancy for a Chadian was fifty years, twenty-eight years fewer than that of the average American.

Sandstone towers on the Ennedi Plateau in Chad. The author led the first climbing expedition to this area in 2010. The team, which included Alex Honnold and James Pearson, climbed the first ascents of twenty towers, leaving thousands more for future generations of climbers.

To get to the Ennedi we had to drive off-road across the Sahara for three long days. About halfway across, in the middle of an endless plain reminiscent of the Bonneville Salt Flats, we came upon a pair of men riding two heavily laden camels. They wore scarves wrapped around their heads, and they just sat there, staring at us, their eyes wide. Then one of the men jumped down, fished a battered tin bowl from his sun-bleached saddlebag, and started milking his camel. When the bowl was half full, he jogged up to our vehicle and offered us the frothy brew. Alex tilted back the bowl and took a glug. We gave them bread and water. When they sauntered off, Alex asked our outfitter, "Who were those guys?"

"They're Toubous," he replied. "They're coming back from Libya. Those bags on the back of the camels are filled with salt and other staples they're taking back to their village."

"Wow," said Alex, slumping back into his seat in the Land Rover. The commitment it took for those guys to set off across the desert with no backup struck all of us.

Alex was traveling more and more for climbing expeditions, and for a kid who had never seen much outside of Sacramento, he was starting to become a global citizen, and his eyes, mind, and heart were open to the vastness of the planet and the people who inhabit different parts of it. In 2012, Alex and I left for a sailing and climbing expedition to the Musandam Peninsula in Oman, where a magical fjorded land on the southern shore of the Strait of Hormuz dazzled us. For three weeks, we explored the area's vast climbing potential—we found hundreds of miles of untouched cliffs lining the shore. We also learned about the Kumzari-speaking people who live in remote fishing villages that can only be accessed by boat. The Kumzari-speaking people are a network of families with their own "pidgin" dialect, a legacy of the cultural collision that has been going on in the area since ancient times. Linguists don't know how their language developed, but it mingles Farsi, Arabic, Hindi, Portuguese, French, Italian, Spanish, and even English. One theory is that the Kumzari-speaking people were originally nomads from the mainland who were pushed out onto the tip of the peninsula by Arab, Yemeni, and Portuguese invaders.

Alex mostly did his own thing while we were there. I'd often run him in to shore in the dinghy in the morning, and I'd watch as he'd wander off to explore a village and then, later, the unexplored cliffs behind the village. No one except Alex knows where he went, whom he met, or how many first ascents he did. But one day he came back to the boat in the evening all excited about a mysterious fortress he found on a high and lonely ridge after a long free solo.

"I can't imagine how they could have built it or what it was for," he mused, with a sparkle in his eye that I had only ever previously seen after he had done a difficult climb.

When he got home from Oman, Alex wanted to use his extra financial resources to start a nonprofit that would somehow make the planet a better place. These expeditions simply and irrevocably changed his view of the world. He told his friend Maury Birdwell of his experiences traveling both in the US and beyond and how they had changed him. Maury, a fellow climber, also happened to be in the business of helping people get nonprofit organizations off the ground.

A few days later, Maury and Alex officially set up the nonprofit. They built a website and a Facebook page and posted their mission statement. It read: "The Honnold Foundation seeks simple, sustainable ways to improve lives worldwide. Simplicity is the key; low-impact, better living is the goal."

What they didn't publicize was the fact that Alex personally seeded the foundation with $50,000—about a third of his income that year—the money his financial adviser had recommended he invest in a mutual fund. "Alex is not the most emotionally expressive person," says Maury. "But he still feels the connection just as strongly as everyone else. He's the kind of person who expresses himself through his actions."

Alex still did not have a specific mission that would "make the planet a better place," but it didn't take long for him to find the perfect fit. Ideally, he wanted something that would help humanity while simultaneously being environmentally friendly.

Not long after they launched the foundation, Alex met a guy named Ted Hesser at one of his talks. At the time, Ted, who is also a climber, was working for a clean energy market research firm in New York City called Bloomberg New Energy Finance. He started sending Alex reports about the growing potential for clean energy. These were twenty- to thirty-page research papers explaining who needed it, where it would work, and who wanted it. The reports were so dense that Ted says most of his clients didn't even read them, let alone understand them. But Alex read them. Carefully. And then he hit Ted with astute questions that, without fail, cut to the heart of what mattered.

Together, Alex, Maury, and Ted found the ideal place for the Honnold Foundation to spend its money wisely. They wanted to make sure they supported technology that would be successful and put it in places that not only needed it but were open and excited for it too. It wouldn't do anybody any good in the long run to spend money in ways that did not coincide with the needs or desires of the communities they were trying to help.

In the beginning, Alex realized that the Honnold Foundation would have its biggest impact in communities where many people still didn't have access to electricity and were looking for it. More specifically, Alex was interested in pay-as-you-go solar systems. Ted, who had been working in the industry for ten years, had already concluded that this very specific slice of the clean energy market had the most potential to create transformative change. "Intellectually, logically, he pieced it together really quickly," says Ted. "It was really impressive."

The Honnold Foundation's first project took place in the Kayenta region of Navajo lands in Arizona. The foundation installed solar panels on homes that had been waiting for years to be connected to the electrical grid. More projects followed, including an expedition to Angola that combined a solar project with the chance for Alex to climb first ascents in a remote mountain range.

Through the Honnold Foundation, Alex was giving away a substantial portion of his personal wealth, and doing so in a meticulously premeditated way, but without any fanfare or hoopla. Maury says that the reason Alex had been low-key about his foundation was because the scale had been too small. "He's trying to hit a really long ball" is how Ted put it.

"Alex has a really interesting relationship with money," says Ted. "Giving away 30 to 40 percent of his income [each year] doesn't mean the same thing to him as it might to someone else. Alex doesn't worry about money the way most people do." Alex is fortunate enough to be able to choose to enjoy a moderate lifestyle, and therefore, he will always have more resources to share with others. He can continue to slowly, methodically, and thoughtfully do his own small part to make the world a better place.

CHAPTER SIXTEEN
Secret Dawn Walls

It was 2014, and Tommy Caldwell and his partner, Kevin Jorgeson, had been climbing the Dawn Wall for eighteen days. They were now a handful of pitches away from completing one of the most difficult rock climbs ever attempted. Tommy first envisioned the climb back in 2007 and began working on it shortly thereafter. Seven years later, his dream of free climbing this magnificent swath of stone on El Cap's southeast face—a route that would become, instantly, the most difficult rock climb on earth—was finally within reach.

Alex arrived at the summit of El Capitan just as Kevin and Tommy were a few hundred feet from topping out. About forty people had gathered to celebrate the momentous occasion. The eclectic ensemble looked like a bunch of groupies gathering backstage after a concert.

There were small patches of ice hidden in the shadows, but overall the air was mild and the sky clear. Climbers were calling it "Juneuary." A couple of cameramen, dangling on ropes at the lip of the cliff, announced that Tommy had just reached the final anchor. But it was located just below the lip in a spot that no one could see. As everyone waited for Tommy and Kevin to scramble up into view, Alex scampered down the steep slab and disappeared over the edge. When Tommy topped out, Alex was right there. They hugged, and Alex hung out while Tommy belayed up Kevin. After congratulating his friends on the climb of their lives, Alex got out of the way. As the cameras whirred, the grizzled, bearded climbers stumbled up the final slab on wobbly legs that hadn't felt solid ground in nearly three weeks. In view of the crowd, Tommy and Kevin stopped and gave each other a hug.

Tommy, who had come down with a cold and lost his voice, appeared bewildered. He embraced his wife awkwardly. It was clear he wasn't comfortable sharing this intimate moment with all these people. He had climbed El Capitan about sixty times, but until now, there had never been more than a friend or two to greet him on top. Kevin, on the other hand, appeared quite comfortable being in the spotlight. He embraced his girlfriend as the paparazzi's flashbulbs popped all around him. Someone handed them bottles of champagne. Tommy popped the cork on his and started drinking it. Kevin shook his up and sprayed it all around as the crowd cheered.

Alex stood in the background quietly observing. Up until this moment, he had been the most famous climber in the world. But not anymore. That title now belonged to Tommy. With access to a strong LTE signal, Tommy and Kevin were using their smartphones to post daily updates from the portaledge at night to their Instagram and Facebook accounts, and news of their climb had gone viral.

It wasn't always like this. In the early part of my climbing career, it was a relief to be able to unplug from the outside world while on expeditions. Back in 1996 I went on an expedition to Baffin Island, and because of the challenges we faced I came home three weeks later than I was supposed to. When I didn't arrive on my flight, my parents, who had driven to the airport to pick me up, had no way of knowing if I was dead or just running late. By 2015, it wasn't just possible for a professional climber to keep their fans updated on their progress in real time, it was expected. For better or worse, social media was now the primary way climbers interacted with each other, and it was how we broadcasted our accomplishments.

John Branch of *The New York Times* got the first interview with Tommy and Kevin when they topped out. Kevin memorably told him: "I think everyone has their own secret Dawn Wall to complete one day, and maybe they can put this project in their own context." He was echoing the same sentiment expressed by Maurice Herzog in the mountaineering classic *Annapurna*: "There are other Annapurnas in the lives of men." Alex stood nearby.

The best climbers, the ones who truly stand out from the rest, the characters who have gone down in history—they've all had at least one magnificent climb that defined them, a route that redrew the boundaries of human potential and set a benchmark for the next generation. The Dawn Wall became Tommy and Kevin's defining moment. Edmund Hillary and Tenzing Norgay had the first ascent of Everest. Reinhold Messner was the first to climb to the top of the world without supplemental oxygen. Warren Harding claimed the Nose. Lynn Hill free climbed the Nose in one day. But Alex didn't yet have one singular accomplishment that defined him, at least not to his own mind. Free soloing Royal Robbins's route on the northwest face of Half Dome couldn't be the end, because there was one more obvious step to take. And there was only one person who had any business even contemplating that next step.

Alex was already known as the world's best free soloist, but he wanted to accomplish something that would cement his legacy. In 1962 Wilt Chamberlain scored a hundred points in a single basketball game, and no one since has come close to this record. Swimmer Michael Phelps won an astonishing eight medals in his second Olympic appearance and went on to win twenty-eight in total . . . more than any other Olympic athlete. In climbing there are no medals. There is usually no cheering crowd. Most feats by climbers and mountaineers go unnoticed by the outside world. Alex wanted nothing less than to redefine the limits of human potential.

What no one, not even his closest friends, knew at the time was that Alex was already well into the process of free soloing El Capitan. Years ago, around the same time that Tommy quietly rappelled off the summit to see if there were enough holds to free climb the Dawn Wall, Alex was making a list of routes he might solo as stepping-stones on his way to the Captain. Each of the routes, in their own way, simulated sections he would face on Freerider, the route up El Cap that he felt offered the best chance of success. El Sendero Luminoso, a 5.12+ in Mexico, which he climbed in January 2014, featured steep technical face climbing like he'd encounter on Freerider's Boulder Problem. The University Wall, 5.12- in Squamish, British Columbia, which he free soloed in August of the same year, had lots of wide cracks and some powerful underclinging, like the moves he'd face on the traverse to the Monster Off-Width.

Alex had worked on the University Wall for several days prepping it for the solo, but he couldn't get it dialed in to the point where he felt good about it. He would later tell me that he got it "to about 95 percent." He always felt that on a solo he should feel at least 99 percent certain of the outcome—

and hopefully with a few .9s tacked on. So he set it aside and moved on to other things. Two and half weeks later, still in Squamish, Alex was having one of those climbing days when everything felt easy. Small holds felt big. His feet felt like they were glued to the rock. He had power to waste. So he walked up to University Wall and started climbing. He had rehearsed an intricate sequence at the crux, which required pinching the bottom of a flake as he carefully tick-tacked his feet along a series of barely perceptible nubs in the rock. These were the moves he was never able to feel quite right about. But when he got to the undercling, he locked off with his right hand and brought his feet up high. As he did, he realized he was feeling so strong that he didn't have to follow the tricky moves he had practiced. Instead, he simply reached high to a good hold above. He would later describe it to me as a moment of "transcendence."

From Squamish, Alex headed to the Needles, a climbing area in the foothills of the Sierras a few hours south of Yosemite. It was here that Alex had set his sights on another route on his list called the Romantic Warrior, 5.12b. He had climbed it eight years earlier and had never forgotten a section called the Book of Deception, a tricky stemming corner at the top of the nine-hundred-foot route. It seemed like a good primer for Freerider's Teflon Corner.

In September, he spent the night in his van in a dirt pullout. The next day he ran laps on the route's crux pitches by rappelling in from above and self-belaying with a small aluminum pulley called a Micro Traxion. The device was designed for hauling bags through caves or up cliffs. It incorporates a ratchet, which holds the load in place while you reset between pulls. In climber parlance this is known as "progress capture." Climbers figured out that Micro Traxions also work well for self-belaying on a fixed strand of rope. We call it "mini-tracking," in reference to the Micro's predecessor, the Mini Traxion, which is bigger and heavier but works in the same way. Alex put a locking carabiner through the small donut hole on the device and clipped it to his harness. As he climbed up the wall, the Micro rolled along the rope at his waist. If he fell, the ratchet, which is lined with tiny angled teeth, would tighten against the rope, holding him in place. The beauty of mini-tracking is that it allows a climber to rehearse a route without needing another person to serve as belayer. This way you're not "wasting someone else's life," as Alex once put it to me.

When Alex got back to his van that evening, he realized he was out of propane, which meant he had no way to cook the only thing he had for dinner—mac and cheese. He debated driving out to get fuel, but it was such a long way to where he could resupply that he might as well bail and head back to Yosemite. Should he just go for the Romantic Warrior route in the morning? It seemed like a bad idea. He had been planning another day or two of rehearsal, because the climbing felt hard and insecure. He stayed the night, and in the morning, while eating an energy bar, in what could be considered a capricious moment of pure motivation and excitement, he said to himself, *Whatever—I'm going for it.*

At the base of the route, he tried to empty his bowels, but nothing happened. This was a bad omen because he usually didn't have any problem going to the bathroom before a big climb. His nerves would loosen up his insides, and it was good to get it out of the way before he was hundreds of feet off the ground. He headed up anyway. The first four hundred feet of the route are relatively easy, and Alex made quick time. But as he approached the first crux pitch, he felt his insides begin to grumble. He was in the middle of a steep pitch, and there were no ledges anywhere. And it would be extremely poor style to go to the bathroom right down the climbing route itself. Alex looked out left, where a flake of rock offered a horizontal handrail. He grabbed it and traversed sideways until he was twenty feet off the side of the route, hanging from 5.10 handholds on an overhanging wall. He slipped his small pack off one arm at a time and shoved it into the crack, then, hanging by his one hand, he pulled his pants down. He brought his legs up into a crouch and "space dumped" into the void. After taking what might have been the most daring poop in history, he cleaned himself up, pulled up his pants, and finished the route in good style. Afterward, he told a couple friends but didn't report the climb or post about it on social media. And he never went back to pose for photos. Alex was keeping this one for himself.

PART THREE
TOPPING OUT

CHAPTER SEVENTEEN
Alex's Amygdala

In December of 2014, Alex, Jimmy, and I gave a lecture at the National Geographic headquarters in Washington, DC, and told stories of our expeditions together, mainly our adventures in Chad and Oman. Afterward, we set up in the reception area to do poster signings. Alex's line stretched out the door, and Jimmy's was nearly as long. Mine was embarrassingly short. A man stepped up to the table behind which I was sitting and identified himself as a neuroscientist. Glancing over at Alex, who was signing posters for his adoring fans, the man leaned in and whispered, "You know Alex's amygdala isn't firing, right?"

The amygdala is an almond-shaped nodule lodged deep in our brains that acts sort of like the hub of a bicycle wheel, with the spokes representing its connection through the limbic system to a vast array of brain structures. The amygdala helps us attach emotional value to stimuli that constantly swirl around us, and it is strongly associated with our most primal emotions like fear. If you've ever felt your pulse shoot up as a result of, say, being badly startled, then you know your amygdala is firing.

I assumed the neuroscientist was speculating that Alex might have Urbach–Wiethe disease, a rare genetic condition that destroys the amygdala. I remembered reading about a famous case of the disease in which brain researchers had anonymously labeled the patient SM-046. The media called her "the woman with no fear." Scientists have been studying her since the mid-1990s in hopes of better understanding fear and anxiety. They've dangled snakes and spiders in her face and had her watch scary movies like *The Blair Witch Project* and *The Shining*. Nothing fazes her.

When I mentioned the neuroscientist's comment to Alex, he scoffed. "That's totally nuts," he said. "I experience fear just like everyone else." Alex had been asked many times whether he's a sociopath or if he has Asperger's, a developmental disorder considered to be a mild form of autism. Alex has conceded that he's probably "somewhere on the autism spectrum." But this was the first time someone had speculated that a basic structure in his brain was defective. And so I wondered if this neuroscientist was asking himself the same question I was: Is Alex Honnold's brain wired differently than the rest of ours, or has he found a way to master life's most primal emotion?

What fascinated me was not the question of whether or not Alex had a working amygdala but instead why everyone, myself included, wanted an explanation for how Alex can do what he does. Anyone who climbs and knows of Alex Honnold's exploits has had the "How does he do it?" conversation. The quest to answer this question has sparked countless magazine articles and blogs, Jimmy and Chai's film, and, yes, this book. I wondered whether this fascination with Alex's brain reveals more about us, the people asking questions, than him. Because for every individual who tips their hat to Alex's talent and nerve, there is another, like the neuroscientist at this event, who wants to label him as abnormal—and perhaps pathologically so.

"People want to explain him away, they want it to be something that doesn't place a demand on them," says J. B. MacKinnon, a writer from Canada who became interested in the amygdala story and arranged for Alex to have a brain scan. "Because if Alex is just an ordinary guy who managed to transform himself into this superhuman figure of fearlessness and cool under pressure, then they should be able to do that too. And nobody wants to believe that's the reality. We all feel this need to make him into something different and unique so the rest of us don't have to take any lessons from what he's done."

"This is something I'm starting to wonder about myself," said Alex when MacKinnon called him and explained he had a neuroscientist lined up to scan his brain. "I don't think I'm abnormal, but I guess we can take a look." Alex knew that he couldn't have Urbach–Wiethe disease, because he did experience fear and always had. Fear made him need to poop before a big solo. Fear gave him high blood pressure before his first public speaking engagements. And fear made his palms sweat when he watched videos of himself free soloing. Still, a seed of doubt had been sown. It would take three days out of his life to travel to South Carolina for a brain scan, but it was a unique opportunity that might lay certain questions to rest and silence those who dismissed him as a freak.

Before shoving him into the MRI machine, Dr. Jane Joseph gave Alex a personality test. Not surprisingly, he scored twice as likely to seek high sensations compared to the average person. But the test also showed him to be well-adjusted emotionally. He scored extremely high in the categories of conscientiousness and premeditation, and low in neuroticism.

But there was one outlier. Joseph had assumed Alex would score low on disinhibition, a term used in psychology to describe the tendency to be impulsive and unaware or uncaring of social customs. A disinhibited person is also likely to be bad at assessing risk. Joseph had assumed that Alex was not overly disinhibited, because if he were, he likely would've already died free soloing. But Alex scored high in this category.

I wasn't surprised, however, knowing what I do about climbing. I see it the opposite way: an inhibited person would never get into free soloing in the first place. But what I find interesting is that while Alex scored high in disinhibition, the test also indicated that he's highly analytical and punctilious—an unusual combination, according to Joseph. This juxtaposition may point to the tension that I've sensed in Alex for a long time, something MacKinnon also noticed. He described Alex to me as someone who is "constantly suppressing some kind of internal intensity."

MacKinnon now stood next to Joseph as the first images of Alex's brain appeared on the monitor. "That's a good-looking brain," she said. Joseph was referring not to the fact that it was extraordinary in any way but that it appeared to be normal and healthy. It didn't have any shrinkage or other signs of degeneration that she often sees in her lab.. Like most brain structures, there are two amygdalae, a right and a left. The ancient Greeks were the first to discover the amygdala when dissecting brains, and the name comes from the Greek word for almond. Joseph told the technician to find Alex's.

A second later it came into focus, deep in Alex's head, not far from the roof of his mouth.

"He has one!" exclaimed Joseph. She couldn't help but be pleased, since she knew very well how serious it would be if his was nonexistent or showed signs of disease. Now it was time to see if she could fire it up.

The test she administered has been used for decades. Subjects are shown a series of pictures that are meant to disturb or excite, and while they are viewing these images, the MRI records any electrical activity that occurs in the brain. Images flashed on the screen in front of Alex's face.

Joseph told me she is loath to view these images even though she has seen them countless times. She admitted that while researching Alex before his arrival, she found herself unable to watch YouTube videos of him free soloing. So at least for a low-sensation seeker, as she describes herself, the images spark strong responses.

The slideshow lasted about fifteen minutes, then Joseph started the second part of the test, which she called the Reward Task. It was a game in which Alex could earn small amounts of money depending on how quickly he pressed the button on a clicker he held in his hand. While Alex clicked away, Joseph monitored a part of the brain called the nucleus accumbens. It's a structure near the top of the brain stem that processes dopamine, a neurotransmitter that carries electrical impulses between neurons. Most people think of dopamine as the chemical associated with motivation and addiction, but its function is complex and still not fully understood. What brain researchers are aware of is that the test Alex was undergoing is known to flood the nucleus accumbens with dopamine in reward-driven people.

When Alex emerged after half an hour in the tube, he looked at Joseph. "I can't say for sure [if my amygdala was lighting up or not], but I was like, 'Whatever.'" It felt, he said, "like looking through a curio museum."

It took Joseph a month to study and prepare the results of Alex's scan. By this point Alex was in China climbing Getu Arch, one of the world's most difficult multi-pitch sport climbs. He was curious about the results, but he had already decided that whatever the brain scan revealed, he was not going to modify his behavior on its account. Joseph had emailed Alex four images: two of his brain and two of a control subject's brain. The pictures showed all activity that had occurred across the entirety of the two tests. The control subject was a rock climber and deemed a high-sensation seeker by the researchers. Alex met him while he was at the university, and Joseph scanned the man shortly after scanning Alex. Joseph made it clear from the start that Alex's scan results were not scientifically valid, because there had only been one control. This was not a study that would be published in any medical journals.

"Is my brain intact?" asked Alex via Skype.

"It's perfectly healthy," said Joseph.

When electrical activity is present in the brain, it shows up on the MRI in varying shades of bright color. The darker the coloring, the more synapses are firing. Areas absent of electrical impulses appear gray. The image of Alex's brain showed two gridlines that formed a plus sign directly over his amygdala. The nodule was dull gray. The MRI had not detected any electrical activity. Neuroscientists call this "zero activation." The only part of his brain that showed any color was the visual cortex—proof that he was actually looking at the images.

Now Joseph referred Alex to the image of the nucleus accumbens taken during the reward task. The results were the same. The neurons weren't firing. Zero activation during both tests was "highly unusual," according to Joseph. The control subject was given the exact same tests. Like Alex, he reported feeling no emotional stimulation. It was obvious to this subject what the game was, and he felt confident that his brain, which had seen him up countless difficult rock climbs, had not taken the bait. He was wrong. His amygdala and nucleus accumbens were both lit up like a Christmas tree.

Those of us who know and follow Alex weren't surprised when we heard the results of the scan. Over the past twenty years, he has focused intently on learning to control fear. It's been a gradual process, something he once described to me as "slowly expanding the bubble around my comfort zone." It's a progression every climber must follow, from first overcoming the irrational fear that ropes and anchors won't hold, all the way to learning how to stay calm and loose when executing difficult moves, even if the fall is dangerous.

Back when he first envisioned free soloing El Capitan, Alex knew that he would need to take this process to a rarified extreme and train himself to control his innate fear response when climbing near the limit of his ability thousands of feet above the ground without a rope. So one possible

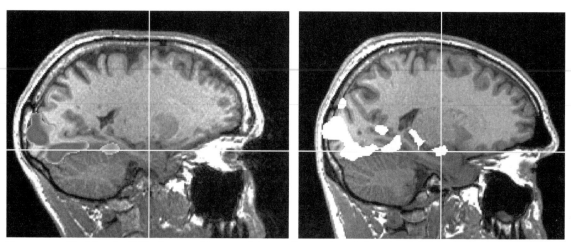

The scan used to determine if Alex has a working amygdala, which is an almond-shaped nodule that helps our brains process fear and other primal emotions. Alex's brain is on the left, a control subject on the right. Crosshairs mark the amygdala. The control subject's amygdala glows, which is indicated by the whiter areas toward the back of the cranium, while Alex's does not.

interpretation of Joseph's findings is that Alex has succeeded brilliantly—assuming, of course, that his amygdala is actually capable of firing, ever. And this, Joseph emphasizes, the test could not determine. It only indicated that his amygdala doesn't respond in the same way to the same stimuli as do those of the vast majority of test subjects that Joseph has studied over the years.

When Alex's book *Alone on the Wall* came out in the fall of 2015, I interviewed him for *National Geographic*. He told me that one of his prime motivators for writing the book was to help people understand why he can do what he does: "I've done so much soloing and worked on my climbing skills so much that my comfort zone is quite large. So, these things that I'm doing that look pretty outrageous, to me they seem normal." He said that it makes "total sense" to him, and that it's "easily understandable," but still, people don't seem to get it. "Maybe I should have explained it better," he said.

He used the analogy of driving on the freeway. It can be terrifying the first time a new driver pulls into speeding traffic from the on-ramp. But as you do it more and more, you become accustomed to the high consequences of a mistake, and after enough repetitions, it's a routine experience, like brushing your teeth.

I pointed out that it's a lot easier to keep your car in the proper lane than it is to hang from a pinky lock on a 5.12 finger crack. But Alex disagreed. He said it's only easy because I've done it a lot. "If you were someone who had *never even seen a car before*, you'd be like, 'Holy [smokes], I'm about to die,'" he said. "Climbing to me is the very same thing. I've actually spent more time climbing than driving. Imagine New York City cabbies and all the outrageous things they do. That's kind of like me with my climbing. I've spent a ton of time hanging on pinky locks, so it's not a big deal."

The rationalization that his free soloing is no more dangerous than being a cabbie in a busy city is one that Alex has carefully constructed, probably because it's the keystone in the story he tells his friends and family to justify the risks he takes. Try to tell him that free soloing is dangerous, and he will argue the point every time. The closest I've come so far is to get Alex to admit that the consequences of a fall while free soloing would be disastrous. But then he'll quickly point out that just because a consequence may be severe, its probability of occurring does not increase. The consequences, he'll say, are equally dire if your hand slips off the steering wheel and you swerve into the other lane and collide head-on with a Mack truck.

Engage Alex in this conversation, as I have on numerous occasions, and invariably he will quote his own homegrown statistic that no free soloist has ever fallen while pushing his limits. "It doesn't seem to be the way that people die," he has said. As far as I know, he is correct. John Bachar died soloing 5.10, which could be considered moderate terrain, at least for him. Derek Hersey, the famed British free soloist who fell off Yosemite's Sentinel Rock in 1993, was on a route rated 5.9. To date, his is the only death ever attributed to free soloing in Yosemite National Park. (Afterward, someone taped a laminated photo of Hersey onto the rock at the start of the route. "We miss you, Derek," it said.) Dan Osman, another free soloist, and a founding member of the North Face team, was killed when his rope broke while practicing a sport he invented called "rope jumping." John "Yabo"

Yablonski, the Stonemaster, and Earl Wiggins, an unsung Colorado climber, both noted free soloists, committed suicide. Charlie Fowler, the Coloradan who on-sight free soloed the Direct North Buttress of Yosemite's Middle Cathedral in 1977, was killed in an avalanche in western China. Michael Reardon drowned off the coast of Ireland. Dean Potter perished while BASE jumping. Henry Barber, who soloed the Steck-Salathe route on Sentinel Rock in 1973 (the same route on which Hersey would later fall), is still alive and well, as is Peter Croft, who, with little fanfare, continues to solo 5.12 at the Owens River Gorge.

"I think that the odds of me actually falling are very low," says Alex. While I might disagree, I see how Alex needs to believe this in order to do what he does. Otherwise, he'd be afraid to do it. And that fear, if it turned to panic at the wrong time, could kill him. Most of us look at our one-in-twenty-four chance of dying in some kind of accident the same way Alex looks at free soloing. We choose to go through life believing that we won't be unlucky, because otherwise we'd be too afraid to get in our cars or even leave the house. If hanging from a fingertip jammed in a crack a thousand feet off the ground is just as ordinary an experience for Alex as negotiating rush-hour traffic is for the rest of us, then one might have to admit that his rationalization makes sense.

I dug deeper into the amygdala question during the months that followed the brain scan, while Alex trained relentlessly for Freerider. I contacted Joseph LeDoux, a neuroscientist at New York University who has been studying the amygdala for thirty-five years. He kicked off the conversation by telling me that writers have a tendency to oversimplify when trying to explain something as complicated as the brain. He said that contrary to popular belief, the amygdala is not the fear center of the brain: "The amygdala has a lot of consequences in the brain that affect our feeling of fear, but the feeling of fear is not generated by the amygdala. . . . The field [of neuroscience] has always failed to make the distinction between fear as an experience and fear as a sort of implicit processing system, and it's caused a lot of confusion." According to LeDoux, damage to the amygdala does not eliminate the conscious experience of fear; rather, it prevents the behavioral and physiological responses to threats—sweaty palms, spiking pulse rate, and tunnel vision.

When I asked LeDoux about the zero activation, he said it was a meaningless result because MRI machines are tuned to detect a certain threshold of electrical activity. "The fact that the experiment failed to find it doesn't mean it wasn't there," he said. He told me that electrodes placed directly onto Alex's amygdala—that is, on the inside of his brain, not the outside—would indeed detect synaptic activity.

And LeDoux dismisses the possibility that Alex's amygdala is dormant. Instead he posits that Alex may have been born with a muted amygdala response relative to the general population, making him a genetic outlier, so to speak. He also says it's likely that Alex has desensitized his amygdala to be less responsive to threats, particularly those associated with a fear of heights, by routinely exposing himself to high places. "By self-exposing, training himself in those situations, he's going to reduce the amygdala activity, because that's what exposure does. And perhaps he has trained himself to be able to turn on that inhibition when he goes into those kinds of situations." In other words, Alex's amygdala has simply gotten used to clinging to the side of cliffs very high off the ground with no backup, in the same way a veteran driver most likely is no longer scared of driving fast on a freeway the way a newly licensed teenage driver might be. Alex has managed to harness his psyche through basic repetitive practices and rational thinking.

CHAPTER EIGHTEEN
The Source

Two years later, in 2016, I landed in Morocco and was going to meet up with Alex, Jimmy Chin, and the entire production crew, who were now in the process of filming what would become the documentary of Alex's epic free solo up El Capitan. They had decided to come to Morocco because Alex had climbed here before and afterward had had one of his best seasons ever in Yosemite.

I traded a Toyota Land Cruiser for a donkey when the road ended at a bustling village called Aguddim. The drive from Marrakech had taken five hours, leading south and east across the flat desert of lowland Morocco up into the High Atlas Mountains. The tarmac followed the ancient path of a historic trans-Saharan caravan route connecting Marrakech with Timbuktu. Beyond Aguddim, there aren't any roads in the most remote parts of the High Atlas, so I proceeded on foot, following a donkey as it clopped along a dusty trail with my green duffel bag strapped to its back.

The muleteer gestured toward a sprawling two-story house surrounded by a tall stone wall. I ducked through a doorway into a courtyard lined with trees and tossed my duffel bag on a wooden bench. A slim, narrow-faced man with light skin emerged from a doorway, gently took my right hand in his, and said, "As-salaamu Alaykum [*peace be unto you*]."

"Wa'alaykumu as-salam [*and unto you peace*]," I returned.

Said Massaoudi, owner of this gîte (French for vacation house), looked to be in his midfifties. He built his guesthouse in 1994, shortly after French and Spanish climbers discovered the gorge's untapped climbing potential. During prime climbing season, March–April and September–October, his guesthouse bustles with foreign climbers, mostly Europeans, who pay 150 dirhams a day (about US$15) for room and board.

I found the team's equipment and other stuff upstairs. One whole wall of a large living room was stacked waist-high in black plastic Pelican cases— hard-sided suitcases that carry camera and film gear. Apparently, the crew was out, because the place was quiet. I poured myself a cup of tea and stepped onto a porch that offered an unobstructed view down the valley through which I had just hiked. A stream ran through the bottom of the valley, and it sparkled in the midday sun. Terraced fields rose from its banks, quilting the surrounding hillsides in varying shades of green—sage, lime, olive, emerald. I could see dozens of snug little Hobbit homes scattered among the lush fields; they were built from mud and dry-stacked limestone blocks that looked like they had grown from the earth like the fig and almond trees that surrounded them. Closer by, a man was spread-eagled in a tree twenty feet in the air whacking walnuts to the ground with a long stick. The air was filled with the sounds of a bustling village: children playing, babies crying, donkeys braying, dogs barking, and insects constantly buzzing. I knew from having studied the Atlas Mountains on Google Earth before the trip that the vast Sahara Desert lay on the other side of the mountains that rose behind the gîte. More desert lay to the north, east, and

One of the many Berber bridges in the Taghia Gorge.

west, but Taghia, fed by a fabled spring called the Source, is an oasis.

The gîte sits in the back of a cirque ringed with red-hued limestone towers that poke into a hazy sky. They call this place the Yosemite of Africa, and for the past two weeks, Jimmy Chin and his crew had been racing around filming Alex and Tommy Caldwell as they raged up the spires that towered above us. A few days earlier, the pair had succeeded on a monster linkup of three of the longest and most difficult routes in the canyon. They were calling it the Taghia Triple Crown. I had arrived a couple days later, in time to spend one day with Tommy before he flew back to the States. Alex was staying on for another week. He told me over the summer that he might "scramble"—a euphemism he often uses for free soloing—one of Taghia's big walls to finish off the trip.

As I sipped a cup of tea in the gîte, Alex appeared in the hallway. I hadn't seen him when I came in and was wondering where he was hiding. Perhaps he'd been in his room all afternoon. He looked around with one eye scrunched shut, said "Hey" and something like "I feel like death," and then shuffled into the bathroom. I'd seen him like this before, suffering from an acute migraine. They don't strike him often, but when they do, it's like Superman and Kryptonite.

I didn't see him again until nine a.m. the next day. "Morning, kiddies," he said. He looked tired, but his face wore a knowing smile, as if he was laughing inwardly at the notion that we were all children and he was the only adult among us. The migraine had passed, and his superpowers were building back up. He placed the book in his hand on a shelf behind the dining table next to the gîte's guestbook. I saw on the binding that it was *Open*, Andre Agassi's autobiography. I hadn't read it but had seen some reviews, and I knew it focused on Agassi's struggles with fame and how he came to hate tennis, the sport that he'd built his life around.

Alex stepped up to the sink attached to the wall outside the bathroom and examined his face in the mirror. Bare-chested and barefoot, he wore only his well-loved black nylon climbing pants. As he stood there brushing his teeth and examining himself in the mirror, I looked around and noticed that every eye in the room was on him. Alex weighs around 160 pounds, which isn't light for a 5'11" rock climber. Every muscle from his waist up is chiseled into his frame. I imagined that punching him in the gut would feel like hitting a wall. His shoulders are broad for the size of his body. He's got unusually long arms and, of course, his famously large hands. His fingers are so thick they actually look buff, like they have miniature muscles in them. And instead of hanging straightish, they appear naturally curled like a gorilla's. His fingernails stand out for being surprisingly well-kept for a climber; most climbers' nails get banged up so badly that at least one or two end up looking like Ruffles potato chips. Mine are sometimes so bad I find myself trying to hide them from certain people. Alex's are scratched, but they're not deformed.

"It's a little embarrassing," said Cheyne Lempe, one of the high-angle cameramen, "but every time I see him, I get a little starstruck." It was true— Alex's natural physical abilities along with his capacity to focus on his goal and work single-mindedly to accomplish it left all of us in awe.

Alex gauging his pump after his free solo of an overhanging 1,800-foot cliff in Taghia, Morocco, called Les Rivières Pourpres. Alex trained in Taghia with Tommy Caldwell before making his first attempt to free solo El Capitan in the fall of 2016.

CHAPTER NINETEEN
Rockfall

On a small ledge at the base of Taoujdad, Alex attached a Micro Traxion to a black rope hanging on the wall. The cliff rose like the prow of a spaceship, seeming to overhang every inch of its 1,800 feet. I followed the rope upward with my eyes, knowing it traced the route Alex planned to free solo. A thousand feet overhead I lost the line where it disappeared above a blocky overhang. On the hike into this valley, the wall had looked reddish in the midday sun, but now that I was standing at its base I saw that its color was closer to orange, with blotchy patches of pink, white, and gray. The route was marked by tiny white splotches—handholds covered in chalk, like a 3D game of connect the dots.

Alex set off with a water bottle and a spare Micro Traxion swinging from a gear loop on the back of his harness. I asked him why he didn't attach the second device as a backup, and he said he thought one was better because it was simpler and cleaner. He'd heard stories of people falling and the two devices jamming against each so that neither clamped down on the rope.

"Get some, Mark," Alex called from above, when he looked down and saw me setting off on my own mini-track adventure. There was a problem though: I hadn't planned to mini-track in Morocco, and so I didn't bring my rig. When Alex invited me that morning to go up with him, I scrounged up some gear, but the devices I was using weren't Micro Traxions. My setup wasn't sliding smoothly up the rope. I had to keep reaching down with one hand to manually pull the rope through the system, which was difficult because the route was steep and unrelenting. I was also missing my head-lamp strap, so if I fell, the devices might jam against each other like Alex had described. The manufacturer's website specifies that the Micro Tra-xion can be used for self-belay, but it should always be backed up in some fashion. Most climbers, myself included, use two. I clip both to my belay loop, but I extend the top one and hold it up by clipping it to a bungee cord (actually an old headlamp strap) around my neck.

The diciest part of mini-tracking is the transition at anchors. This requires clipping a lanyard to the anchor to secure myself, then removing the device from the lower rope and putting it back on the rope above. There is no room for error, and mistakes made at these changeovers have resulted in a number of fatal accidents.

I hadn't warmed up, and there were no rests. And even if I had, the route was above my current ability. By the time I was 120 feet up, my forearms were burning. I pumped out on the second pitch, meaning my arms got so tired that my fingers opened and let go of the holds against my will. I fell back on the rope. As I hung there and shook out my arms, all I could think about was the horror of pumping out while free soloing. I knew the climb-ing was easy for Alex and that this would never happen, but still, thinking about it made me slightly nauseated. I was also skeptical of the integrity of some of the holds I was pulling on. A few were nothing more than con-gealed blobs of calcite that had leached out of the limestone. I yanked on one of them while I was hanging there, and it felt solid, but I knew that some holds, especially on limestone, feel secure right up until they break off. We call them "time bombs."

I hung on the rope or fell at least once on most of the pitches, but I eventually worked out the kinks with my rig, and there were sections that I climbed well. It was thrilling to be high off the deck in Morocco, pulling hard on small holds. At the anchor of the sixth pitch, about halfway up the route, I met Alex, who was on his way down. He had climbed the entire route in about ninety minutes.

A few days later, Jimmy was high on the same wall, preparing to film Alex's free solo ascent, and like always, he hooked his daisy chain to the two-bolt anchor, unhooked his rappel device from the black static line he had just slid down, and shifted his weight onto the tether. "OFF," he yelled, the signal that the rope was free, and Mikey Schaefer, his most trusted cameraman, could then come down. Jimmy secured himself to the next rope, transitioned off the anchor, disconnected his daisy chain, and started rappelling down the next rope. The rock was gray and weathered, slightly less than vertical. Jimmy walked down the wall, carefully placing his feet so as to avoid any loose rocks.

When French sport climbers first established Les Rivières Pourpres and other routes snaking up this vast acreage of limestone cliff, they rappelled the route from above to inspect, clean, and protect it. In addition to placing a dotted line of expansion bolts for anchoring ropes, they pried off any loose blocks and flakes of rock that might pose a danger while climbing. It's standard practice when establishing bolted routes and creates a relatively safe climbing experience for both the first ascensionist and all other subsequent climbers. Jimmy's crew had figured out camera positions off to the side of the route so they could film Alex as he climbed past. These sections of rock, well beyond arm's reach of the route, had never been touched, let alone scoured for loose rock. Dislodging a deadly missile onto a fellow cameraman—or even Alex himself—was always a real and nerve-fraying possibility and one Jimmy was careful to avoid at all times.

So Jimmy couldn't believe it when he looked down and saw a backpack-sized block sliding out from under his right foot. The terrifying sound of rock grating against rock filled the air. There was nothing he could do to stop what was about to happen. Two of his close friends, Dave Allfrey and Jim Hurst, were somewhere down below.

"ROCK, ROCK, ROCK," he bellowed. The boulder bounced several times, leaving puffs of dust each time it hit the wall and filling the air with a loud cracking that reverberated through the canyon. Spinning violently, it hit a grassy terrace sixty feet below, where it exploded and dislodged several more rocks. Jimmy looked down and watched two dozen softball- to football-sized rocks raining down toward Dave and Jim.

Four hundred feet below, Dave heard the cracking and the call of "ROCK" that is every climber's nightmare. He sucked himself in close to the wall and tried to make himself as small as he could under his helmet.

The next thirty seconds passed in slow motion for Jimmy. He heard the rocks hit the canyon floor, then an eerie silence. The radio crackled to life. "I'm okay," said Dave, "but holy [cow] was that close." Jim came on the line and said he was also okay.

Jimmy hung on the rope, his hands over his face. "This is so [messed up]," he muttered.

▲▲

Later that day, at the top of the wall, after Alex had successfully topped out, Jimmy turned to me and said, "Today was awful for me. The thing is, I was hyper-focused. I knew the most dangerous thing that could happen would be to kick off a rock. It was all I was thinking about. The place I put my foot, fifteen people had already gone over that ground. It kind of made me lose my stomach. I told Mikey, 'The last thing I want to do right now is shoot somebody soloing.'"

"And I had to be like, 'Hey, he will be up here in thirty minutes. You got a job to do. Put it in your pocket and think about it later,'" said Mikey.

"This stuff is gnarly," said Jimmy. "And I knew it would be like this—I mean, I knew it would be dangerous like everything else we do. But with this many cameramen, the chances of hurting someone else . . ." His voice trailed off and he looked down at the ground, which was covered in loose rocks.

Any climber who ventures out of the gym or beyond manicured sport-climbing crags has had close encounters with rockfall. It's part of the game and a risk you learn to mitigate rather than eliminate. When I'd heard Jimmy say that he'd knocked off a rock above Jim and Dave, I wasn't surprised. It is a common occurrence. I've had my bell rung at least a dozen times by golf ball–sized rocks that have taken chunks out of many helmets I've owned over the years. But I've always been roped in when this happened.

The real reason this incident was so chilling was because we all knew that it could happen when Alex was on the wall. Without the security of a rope, he can't squeeze in tight, dive for cover, or shield his head with his arms. And he doesn't wear a helmet because it would be useless if he fell from any appreciable height. My stomach churned as I imagined a shower of rock shrapnel peppering him during a hard sequence. I know what it feels like to get whapped with a small piece of stone. Even a peanut-sized rock hitting Alex in the head might cause him to falter if it happened at the wrong moment.

I had been through a lot of emotional, pressure-packed moments with Jimmy over the years, but I had never seen him like this before. Dave said afterward that he could feel the rush of wind on his ears as watermelon-sized chunks of rock came within inches of his skull. Yes, he was wearing a helmet, but it wasn't going to offer much in the way of protection against rocks that big, which would have ripped his head off his body. Jimmy was now bearing the full weight of his decision to take on this job. Before Jimmy decided to make the film, he had asked his friend Jon Krakauer, author of the bestselling book *Into Thin Air*, what he thought. Krakauer gave him the perfectly rational response that someone would film Alex and that Jimmy should be the guy because he was the most qualified to do it. But at that moment, this justification seemed utterly worthless, like "somebody's going to jump the Grand Canyon in a rocket car, so it might as well be you."

In Jimmy's film *Meru*, he has a line about how the best alpinists are the ones with the worst memories. Only those who can selectively forget the misery and near misses are willing to return again and again to attempt big dangerous climbs. While this project didn't involve the physical discomfort of a Himalayan expedition like Meru, it certainly had its own set of horrors.

We all just sat there, listening to the wind whistle through the notches in the rock, staring off at the parched hills surrounding the tiny oasis of Taghia. "I don't want to do this job for the rest of my life," said Mikey. "All the stress is just going to ruin me. I've seen other shooters that work in the mountains, and they've seen it go bad, and now they're paranoid, because they hit their threshold. And you know, this job doesn't even pay that well. We could be doing car commercials or shooting models in Mexico, and we'd get paid so much more." Mikey paused and appeared to be deep in thought, like he was imagining those bikini-clad models on the beach. I looked at Jimmy, and he was finally smiling. He has a house in Mexico, and he does photo shoots with supermodels on occasion. "But none of that work is really meaningful," Mikey added. "You're just selling shit. Here we're actually trying to show somebody special."

Later, back at the gîte, everyone hung out on the roof watching the sunset. All that was left of the trip was to pack up and head home. It would have been the perfect time to break out some beers to celebrate, but Alex and Jimmy don't drink, and consuming alcohol outside of a licensed bar is against the law in the Kingdom of Morocco. After Les Rivières Pourpres, Alex had gone and soloed a classic multi-pitch 5.11. In total, he had soloed an El Cap's worth of hard rock. It had been one of the most impressive days of free soloing in the history of the sport. Alex wasn't glowing and animated like I'd seen him after other big successful days though—too much hadn't gone well for everyone. But he was more chatty than usual, and a question I'd been pondering came to mind.

I wondered where Alex put his odds of success if he decided to go for it. It's a pretty loaded question to ask someone, but given his mood and the tie-in to the book, I decided to toss it out.

"I'm looking for something repeatable," said Alex. In other words, he wasn't willing to roll the dice and hope they came up with the right number.

He needed to be sure he could do it—otherwise, he just wasn't willing to take the chance.

When Jimmy and I first started talking about this project, he suggested I join his crew as a rigger and work alongside Dave helping fix anchors and ropes for the cameramen. At first, I loved the idea, because it would intimately embed me in the crew. But I've done a lot of rigging over the years, and I fully understand the dangers involved. When I stepped back and thought about it carefully, contemplating all the loose rock, the sharp edges, and how much danger I'd already exposed myself to in my life, I decided it wasn't worth the risk.

In 2008, not long after an expedition to Kashmir, I retired from high-risk Himalayan expeditions. I let go of my desire to compete with the best alpinists and adventurers of my generation—an ambition that's burned in me since I was a kid. I continued to climb, ski, and travel the world. I just did so with a greater sense of safety than before.

There have been several times over the years I've known Alex that I've wanted to grab him by the shoulders and say, "Dude, if you don't step back from the edge, you're gonna miss out on a lot of good living." I felt that same impulse on the rooftop in Taghia.

Instead, I said, "There are a lot of things that you still need to experience, Alex."

But for Alex, it was uncomplicated. I interviewed him for the National Geographic Adventure Blog back in 2015 and asked him the "why" question everyone wants to know. He simply said, "Why does anyone have a hobby or a passion? It's because I find meaning and fulfillment in it, it's beautiful, and I enjoy it."

CHAPTER TWENTY
The Beastmaker

In October of that same year we were all back in Yosemite for the main event. This time I had brought along my wife, Hampton, and our seven-month-old son, Tommy. I was now on assignment for *National Geographic* magazine, which was also the main sponsor of Jimmy and Chai's film.

Alex had already been there for a couple weeks by the time I arrived. I texted him to find out where he was, and he replied, Come say hi. I'm hang-boarding at Mike's.

We found then–Yosemite National Park chief of staff Mike Gauthier's house. In recent years, Mike had given Alex permission to park his van in his driveway, which was unique considering the Park Service's chronically strained relationship with the climbing community.

Mike's home is a one-story ranch with a large garage attached. A fire pit and a weathered picnic table sit in the middle of a yard that has been left to grow wild. I could see sections of upper Yosemite Falls through the massive oak trees growing all around the house. California was in the midst of a record-breaking drought, and the waterfall was barely a trickle. Normally, the falls' roar fills the valley, but on this day it was silent.

We found Alex sitting in his van. "Hey, Hampton," he said, giving my wife a hug. Alex took Tommy's tiny hand—about the size of one segment on

Alex's index finger—and gave it a shake. "Nice to meet you, Thomas," he said, looking our little man in the eye with a bemused smile. "Welcome to my home," he said proudly, gesturing toward the interior of his Dodge Pro-Master 2500. In the back of the van, there was a futon set on a wooden frame about three feet above the carpeted floor. Underneath was a storage area where he kept his climbing gear in crates. There was a bookshelf above the bed that was about two-thirds full. It was dark back there, so I couldn't quite make out the titles, but I recognized several guidebooks to Yosemite and the Sierras, and I guessed that the rest were probably environmental nonfiction, the subject Alex was currently most passionate about. Across from the door, a countertop ran from the edge of the bed to the back of the driver's seat. It housed a propane range with a double-burner stove top and a small oven below. "My friends convinced me I should have an oven," he explained, "but I don't know, I'm not much of a baker." A small sink without a faucet was adjacent to the stove, and there was a mini fridge beneath it. Cabinets made of blond hardwood hung above and below the countertop. The handles were different colored lobes from Black Diamond Camalots—a type of camming device. Alex had hired his friend and climbing partner Mason Earle to customize the interior, and he'd added this eye-catching detail.

Alex was passionate about living in the simplest manner possible. While to some, a van may seem limiting, cramped, and maybe a bit lonely, for Alex it allowed him to be razor-focused. He didn't have utility bills to worry about every month, furniture to buy, or any of the other stuff that adults are in charge of. All he had to do was wake up and figure out where he was going to climb that day, what crag he wanted to spend time at, or what kind of a workout he needed to accomplish to continue to stay strong and perfect his craft.

Perhaps the van's most distinctive feature was the hangboard bolted above the door. Two feet wide and eight inches in height, it was routed from a single piece of yellow poplar featuring variously sized grips intended for finger strengthening. *Beastmaker 2000* was branded into the wood in the upper right corner. "Check out these 45-degree slopers," he said, fingering two ramp-like grips on the top of the board. I reached up to feel them. They were baby-bottom smooth, with nowhere to grab. "Supposedly there are humans that can hang these," he said, "but I'm skeptical." All the holds on the Beastmaker are designed to mimic the features a climber might find on real rock. On the outside of the bottom row are the "monos"—two divots just big enough for the tip of one finger. Rumor has it that Adam Ondra can do a one-arm pull-up on this tiny pocket.

Alex looked down at his phone. Beastmaker has an app that offers different workouts. The one Alex was doing was called the Beasty. To complete it, Alex had to hang from the board, off and on, for ninety minutes. He was proving that his climbing and his fitness were his main focuses. It didn't matter if he had friends over or if there was some other event happening elsewhere. It was his time to work out, and he needed to be consistent. He never failed. As we chatted, the app was counting down a two-minute interval between sets. When the timer hit 00:00, the background on the app turned from green to red.

"Time for my next burn," he said, stepping up to the board and gripping a half-inch-wide ledge on the bottom row of holds with the fingertips on his right hand. He settled onto his fingers, lifted his feet in the air, and reeled himself upward with one arm. At the top, with his chin even with the bottom of the board, his head nearly touching the ceiling, he locked off for a couple seconds, then slowly lowered himself back down. Climbers call this a "one-armed negative," and before that moment I had never actually seen someone do one.

"I'm glad you guys came by," he said, stepping back into the van. "These workouts are pretty boring, so it's nice to have people to chat with between burns."

He reached for a journal with a black cover sitting on the counter and jotted down some symbols to denote the set he had just cranked off. He explained that he has different symbols for the various holds on the board. I looked over his shoulder as he flipped through a few pages. The book was filled with what looked like hieroglyphics. For years, Alex has been meticulously recording everything that he does related to climbing. He keeps track of every route—how long it took, little notes on how it felt—plus the details of every training session, including every exercise of every hangboard set. "I've got stacks of these notebooks at home," he told us, "going back to around 2004."

"Is it actually useful to record all that info?" I asked.

"Believe it or not, I do look back on it occasionally, and I can see how much I'm improving—or not." He put down the book, opened the mini fridge, and pulled out some hummus and a loaf of bread. "And I've been making progress. Earlier in the summer I couldn't even hang the L3 chisel, but now I can."

There are two things Alex trains to improve his prowess on the rock:

power and endurance. The latter is something that he has in almost unlimited supply, and he maintains it by running, going on long hikes, and soloing and simul-climbing a mind-numbing number of pitches every week. He once free soloed a hundred pitches in a morning—that's more than the average weekend warrior climbs in a year. His legendary endurance is a big part of what sets him apart from other climbers. And it's what has allowed him to climb things like the Yosemite and Taghia Triple Crown. Tommy Caldwell is the only climber I know who can keep up with him in the endurance arena.

What Alex lacks, at least to his own mind, is power, or what climbers call "contact strength." The ability to hang on tiny holds hinges on two things: the thickness of finger and forearm tendons and the ratio of this tendon strength to body weight. This type of strength can be trained and increased, as Alex's black books bear out, but just like the ability to run fast or jump high, if you're not born with unusually strong tendons, you will never rock climb at an elite level. As a climber, Alex is naturally gifted, probably more so than 99 percent of the population, but his maximum grade of 5.14c is still a full tier below the highest echelon of climbing, where the grades top out at 5.15d. The difference between sport climbing and the big wall linkups that Alex specializes in is like the difference between sprinting and distance running. One relies primarily on power, the other on endurance. Alex is a long-distance thoroughbred, not a sprinter, and no matter how hard he trains, he will never be able to pull as hard as the world's best sport climbers—guys like Chris Sharma, Adam Ondra, and Alex Megos—just like how Haile Gebrselassie will never beat Usain Bolt in the hundred-meter dash. The point is that while sport climbing and big walls are part of the same sport, they're entirely different disciplines. One of the things that makes climbing unique, though, is that the different disciplines can be combined. The Dawn Wall, which combines powerful cutting-edge sport climbing with the drawn-out effort of a medieval siege, is a perfect example. Tommy Caldwell told me in Morocco that in 2014 he invited Alex to join him on the Dawn Wall when Kevin Jorgeson got hurt. But Alex declined because he didn't think he was strong enough. "I've only climbed 5.14c," he told Tommy, "so how do you expect me to climb 5.14d up on El Cap?"

"I think Alex was selling himself short," Tommy told me. "He could do it. I'm just not sure if he has the attention span for something like the Dawn Wall."

Since I first met Alex, he has always been quick to point out climbers that can crank harder than him: "You know Alex Megos did Realization in one afternoon, right? That's just sick." (Realization is widely regarded as the world's first 5.15a, established by Chris Sharma in 2001.) It bothers Alex that he's lauded as one of the world's best rock climbers when there are teenagers popping up in climbing gyms all over the country who can pull harder than he can. Earlier in the year he recounted a story of getting burned off by a fourteen-year-old girl at an indoor climbing center in Denver: "I was like, wow, I can't climb that route. I wish I could climb as hard as that girl." He routinely gets questions about whether he will compete in the first Olympic climbing competition, which will take place in Tokyo. But Alex is keenly aware of what he is—and is not—capable of. "People don't get it," he said. "I just can't perform at that level."

After a few more sets, the app said it was time for a longer break, so Alex sat down on the floor with his back against the cabinet and ate his sandwich.

CHAPTER TWENTY-ONE
Tommy Weighs In

It was nine thirty in the morning, and the valley was soaked from a downpour the night before. Tommy Caldwell and I sat in camp chairs in one of the only dry spots we could find, beneath a fifteen-foot-tall egg-shaped rock called the MSG Boulder. The overhanging face rising above the backs of our camp chairs proffered a difficult boulder problem that Tommy had climbed a few years ago. From where I sat, I could finger the first hold, which was caked white with climber's chalk.

El Capitan, the granite monolith around which all our lives seemed to rotate, was visible through the widely spaced lodgepole pines that grew from the wet, loamy earth. The cliff was slicked with water, its sides gleaming. Mist rose from the meadow beneath it. Between El Cap and where we sat was Ribbon Falls, which spills from an alcove on a 1,500-foot cliff just west of El Capitan. It was pumping from the recent rain, which filled the air with soothing white noise.

Tommy and his family were leaving Yosemite that afternoon, and I asked him if we could chat about Alex. I was curious to find out how he was feeling about our mutual friend's daring plan now that he'd had more time to think about it.

Alex had fallen on the Freeblast (the lower ten pitches of Freerider) two weeks earlier and sprained his ankle. All of his plans were now up in the air.

But despite the pain and swelling, he was back climbing now, a sneaker on the hurt foot and a rock shoe on the other. Alex called Tommy after the fall to tell him about it.

I asked Tommy if Alex falling (with a rope) on the route that he was intending to climb free solo made him feel like he should try to talk Alex out of it. If he could fall while wearing a rope, obviously he could fall when he didn't have one.

"I don't really feel like it's my role to talk him out of it. Part of me wants him to do this thing that's obviously very important to him. And if I were in his situation, I don't know if I could not try it. On the other hand, I think that him falling is a real possibility. And I haven't let myself go there. I went and climbed the Freeblast the other day partly because I was just curious how it would feel to free solo it. Every time I have climbed that part of El Cap, I've kind of felt lucky to get through it. I'm like, 'Wow, I didn't slip.'"

"What do you think is driving him to do this?"

"I think he is driven by mastery. He listens to soundtracks of superhero movies and stuff like that," said Tommy, chuckling. "He likes to envision himself as this larger-than-life superhero. Which he kind of is."

"What about the film? Do you think it's putting pressure on him?"

"I grew up in this world where filming and publicizing things was very much looked down upon," replied Tommy. "It was supposed to be about the purity of the climber in the landscape, and you didn't want to project outside of that. But I have also grown up taking part in competitions, and I understand the appeal. And I think each younger generation veers more toward being motivated by that side of things. Alex would be trying to free solo El Cap regardless of whether it was being filmed or not, but I'm sure that being filmed is a motivator for him, and quite possibly a really positive motivator. It gets him excited because I think a lot of the appeal is wanting to look like a superhero to the masses—and that's not going to happen without a film. If you look at people like Peter Croft and the free soloists of the past, they did it under that old-school ethos. They didn't tell anybody about it, and the people in that world admired them for that, while people outside of that world didn't really care, because they didn't know it was happening. I think Alex wants everybody to care."

Tommy may be the only person who can keep up with Alex in the mountains, but there's one thing he won't do: climb without a rope. From an early age, his father drilled into him the family ethic of avoiding needlessly reckless pursuits. And by "needlessly reckless" he meant two specific types of climbing: Himalayan alpinism and free soloing.

"I'd be curious to know if there's any free soloist who has a family with a strong mountain background. It's almost easier to have a family that is oblivious to the whole thing," says Tommy.

The wisdom of his dad's edict has played itself out over the years. Tommy says he can think of at least ten times that he has fallen unexpectedly while climbing. Alex says he's never fallen unexpectedly, but Tommy points to several instances when he has done precisely that, including the last climb they did in Morocco. Alex was following Tommy's lead when he broke a hold on a 5.10 pitch and fell. When Tommy called him on it, Alex said, "If I were free soloing, I would never have grabbed that hold."

"Maybe that's true," Tommy says, "but what if he didn't recognize that it was a loose hold? I once had a bad fall on El Capitan where the sole of my shoe just ripped off."

In 2012, while descending from a marathon linkup of nine peaks on Patagonia's Fitz Roy Massif, Tommy and Alex were discussing a familiar topic among all climbers: Were the risks worth the reward? Tommy told Alex that his risk calculus had changed since he became a father—he'd become more conservative as a climber. Alex replied bluntly that Tommy's family "would be fine without him." Tommy wasn't offended; Alex has no children, and he comes from a family that supposedly never used the "L" word (love). Tommy understood the remark as perhaps reflecting Alex's own view of himself, that he wouldn't be unduly missed if he died soloing, and a sign that his risk calculus hasn't changed over the years.

Later, Tommy and Alex were crossing a glacier unroped when Alex fell into a crevasse. For a few seconds, Tommy thought Alex might be lost somewhere in the bowels of the glacier. Had his best friend just died right in front of him? Then Alex climbed out of the hole and started giggling. "I was like, 'Hmmm,'" says Tommy. "Something's not quite right about this guy."

CHAPTER TWENTY-TWO
The Rostrum

The ground was still wet in Foresta the next morning, so I figured Alex would take the day off from climbing. But by midmorning the sun was shining, and the ground seemed to be dry. I was buzzing from multiple cups of coffee, and I got this strange feeling that I might be missing something important. Because I was not part of the film production crew, I wasn't aware of their plan that morning. I texted a couple people, but no one responded. So I tried Jacob, one of the cameramen.

> **Where are you guys?**
> Rostruming.
> **Is he doing it?**
> Yes.

I frantically threw some climbing gear into my pack while Hampton got Tommy into his car seat. We arrived at the pull-off above the Rostrum on Highway 41 half an hour later. I climbed over the wall and wandered down a weathered slab, taking care to avoid the wet patches. The rock was pockmarked with nooks and crannies, most of which were filled with water. As the slab dropped away, the summit of the Rostrum came into view, where half a dozen people were tinkering with a giant camera crane perched at the lip of the cliff. Alex, wearing a bright red shirt, waved, as did a couple of the other guys. I worked my way toward the lip of a six-hundred-foot north-facing cliff that sits adjacent to the Rostrum, looking for a place to watch the climb from. I could see most of the route called Excellent Adventure from where we sat. Alex would climb all of the 5.11 North Face route (often just called the Regular Route or, in a confusing same-name description as the cliff itself, the Rostrum) as a warmup leading to the 5.13 variation at the top. I couldn't see any of the Regular Route because it was hidden around a corner, but I knew it would only take Alex forty-five minutes or so to dispatch with the lower six pitches. For whatever reason, Alex had chosen the Excellent Adventure as his stepping-stone to his El Capitan free solo. It was his test for whether he was ready for the main event.

Above the summit and a few miles to the northwest I could see the burnt meadows of Foresta, and as I strained to spot the cabin where we had been staying, my eye was drawn to the thousands of orange ponderosa pines that lay scattered across the surrounding hills. The National Forest Service estimates that sixty-six million trees died across the Sierra Nevada as a result of the severe drought that plagued California from 2010 to 2016. A third of those trees had died just in the last year. The groundwater had dried out, and the lack of it had weakened these majestic trees, leaving them susceptible to an infestation of pine beetles. I had just seen a bulletin about the pine beetle on a message board down in the village. It said that if the drought continued, every ponderosa in the Sierra Nevada would eventually die.

A few minutes later, Alex's silhouette appeared on the edge of the buttress, fifty feet below the Excellent Adventure. Before scrambling down to this vantage point, I briefly debated not watching him at all. Alex had free soloed a route called the Great Escape a couple of days earlier, and it was a distressing experience. But however unnerving it was to watch Alex free solo firsthand, I knew that as a reporter for *National Geographic* I needed to witness it. As soon as Alex came into view, it was obvious that today something was different. Perhaps it was my position, which offered a stunning bird's-eye perspective of a man laying down all his chips for the chance to walk on the razor's edge between life and death. It felt different to be watching from above instead of from the ground—where he'd land if anything went wrong. But there was something else, and as Alex stemmed up the overhanging corner below the roof, I realized what it was: the herky-jerky, pained movement I had witnessed on the Great Escape was gone, replaced by a relaxed and proficient smoothness. Alex had found the flow, he was having fun, and the climbing appeared easy—despite the fact that it was not.

With his legs split wide, bridged between the pages of the granite open book, he made a long reach with his right hand to a horizontal flake above him. Every other climber that had scaled this route since the moves were first deciphered by Peter Croft and Dave Shultz seventeen years ago had placed a camming device in the crack created by the flake to establish a fail-safe anchor point. Alex, however, would simply trust his continued existence to the four fingers on his right hand and nothing else.

But if Alex was carrying the psychological weight of knowing that his life hung eight hundred feet in the air from a few bits of flesh and bone, he didn't show it. Instead, he dangled from the plate of rock by one arm, taking his time. I could see green forest filling the gap formed between his horizontal red-shirted body and the gray slab of rock from which his slender human form was suspended.

And then, in the middle of what may have been one of the boldest feats of athleticism ever, Alex did something that was surprising, casual, arrogant, and inspiring all at the same time. He reached down with his free hand to adjust his shirt where it had bunched up under the strap of his chalk bag. He hung there for far longer than was necessary, until finally, like a coiled spring, he surged over the 90-degree lip of the roof to a fingertip edge that he latched with his left hand. With his arms fully stretched to their greatest extent, he smoothly drew his legs over the lip like a cobra rising from a snake charmer's basket. Now there was nothing left but forty feet of heroic jamming up the final crack that sliced the gray shield of rock guarding the summit.

When he topped out, Alex stood at the cliff's edge, his heels inches from the void. He didn't yell or even speak, but his head bobbed up and down as if he was nodding affirmatively. I flashed back to a YouTube video of Dean Potter free soloing Heaven in 2006. At the time it was probably the hardest free solo ever done in Yosemite. He had rehearsed it for weeks. When he pulled over the lip, Dean went ballistic. Fists balled, every muscle in his body flexed, he screamed at the top of his lungs like a Viking warrior. Alex, in contrast, just stood there silently. The only noticeable thing he did was hold his arms out in front of him, like a weight lifter admiring his muscles after a difficult set. It was something I'd seen him do many times, but I couldn't tell if it was vanity or if he was examining the thickness of the blood-engorged veins in his forearms as a way to gauge how pumped he had gotten, which is to say how hard he had pushed himself.

"You saw all that, right?" said Jimmy, slapping me a high five when I arrived on top a few minutes later.

"Uh, yeah," I replied, looking directly at Alex, who was sitting a few feet away. "It was only the sickest thing I've ever witnessed in my life." I took a step toward Alex and clasped his hand. "Nice work, my man."

"Thanks, dude." His brown eyes were wide open and twinkling. His mom had once described them as "cow eyes," and they are that big, but a cow would never look at you the way Alex was looking at me right then. He was a man, stripped of all the protective layers we wear to shield us from the world. The smile he wore was so big and so genuine that it gave him an aura, a glow I had only seen on him a few times since I'd known him. Once was after he set the hook pitch in Borneo, another was when he climbed the underside of a sandstone arch in Chad. And I'd seen it a third time, in the five-minute film of him soloing El Sendero Luminoso in Mexico. He was high on the wall, hanging from a fingertip edge, when he looked back over his shoulder at a drone hovering in the air behind him. The look on his face—it's the joy of knowing that life cannot be experienced more fully.

Peter Croft once explained the feeling you get from free soloing as "a heightened type of perception. A little edge that you need to stand on looks huge—everything comes into high relief. That's just what happens to your body and your mind when you're focused intensely on the feedback you're getting from the environment and there are no other distractions.

You become an instinctive animal rather than a person trying to do a hard climb, and that perception doesn't immediately go away when you get to the top. It dulls over time, but for a while it feels like you almost have super senses. Everything is more intense—the sounds of the swifts flying around or the colors of the sun going down. A lot of times I don't want to go down, I don't want it to end."

"You weren't here when I topped out," said Alex. "But I was really fired up. I think that's the best solo I've ever done."

"Sort of the opposite of Morocco, huh?" I said.

"Yeah, totally. I felt really good on this one."

Maybe that's all any of us need to know. Maybe we're all guilty of ruthlessly overanalyzing Alex's motivations—like we do our own. Perhaps Alex is simply trying to "live deep and suck out all the marrow of life," as Henry David Thoreau wrote in *Walden*.

Jimmy and I looked at each other, and I knew we were both thinking that if Alex could free solo the Excellent Adventure and feel this good, he could—and he would—free solo Freerider up El Cap. Though no one said it, we sensed Alex would attempt his magnum opus—soon.

CHAPTER TWENTY-THREE
Going for It

It was now November, and Thanksgiving was just around the corner. The weather was getting colder, and as winter approached, the window for Alex's climb was getting smaller and smaller. Alex was climbing well, even though he'd been injured earlier in the season, and by now, he'd checked off all the free solos on his list of training goals. He felt ready, and the climb was set to begin in less than twelve hours.

Peter Gwin, then the expeditions and adventure editor at *National Geographic* magazine, arrived in the park to help me break the news of Alex's historic climb. That night we were sitting at the kitchen table in my cabin hard at work on the story that we planned to break within minutes of Alex topping out on Freerider. Alex's impending ascent had been one of the best-kept secrets in the history of the sport, but since *National Geographic* had the exclusive, and we'd all been working on this project for months, everyone was worried that someone might scoop us. I worried most about John Branch, the sports reporter for *The New York Times*, who won a Pulitzer in 2013 for his story about the deadly Tunnel Creek avalanche in Washington State and wrote a feature about the Dawn Wall; he lives just a few hours from Yosemite in San Francisco. I knew he would be following Adam Ondra's attempt to make the second free ascent of the Dawn Wall, which was all over social media, and it seemed like only a matter of time before one of his contacts in Yosemite spilled the beans about what Alex was up to.

By now, virtually all of the core Yosemite climbers knew that Alex was going to free solo Freerider. There were five different teams on the cliff attempting to free climb the route, and it must have been obvious to them what was going on: Alex Honnold, being filmed by Jimmy Chin and Mikey Schaefer, rehearsing the crux pitches of Freerider, a route he had already done multiple times. Why else would he be doing that if not to prep for the free solo? It was well known in the climbing community that Alex had been eyeing this prize for years.

We were making our final edits to the different versions of the story we had already written, much like we had when breaking other outdoor industry news. But this was different.

I was sitting at the small kitchen table. Peter sat across from me on the couch, his computer in his lap. I knew it was coming.

"Hey, I hate to bring this up, but we need to talk about what we write if Alex falls," Peter said.

The editors at *National Geographic* had discussed this gut-wrenching scenario at length and even debated whether or not to cover Alex's attempt. Would it be seen in some quarters as promoting dangerous behavior? Could it be construed as people wanting to watch something despite a potentially horrific outcome simply for entertainment's sake or morbid curiosity? Ultimately, they concluded that—just as *National Geographic* had covered the first ascent of Mount Everest in 1953 (which many at the time considered an unnecessarily reckless endeavor) and many other dangerous climbing expeditions—if Alex was going to attempt to free solo El Capitan, *National Geographic* was going to cover it, whatever the outcome.

But Peter and I hadn't really discussed exactly what we'd say if it ended tragically. I had thought about it and decided that trying to file a news story in the moments after watching a friend's death would be something I couldn't do. "I'm sorry, man, but I can't go there."

"It's okay," he said. "I wrote something on the plane." A minute later an invitation to a Google doc popped up in my email. The first line read:

> YOSEMITE NATIONAL PARK—Renowned climber Alex Honnold died Tuesday after he fell while attempting to become the first person ever to scale the iconic 3,000-foot granite wall known as El Capitan without using any ropes or other safety gear.

I couldn't read any further.

At 2:57 a.m., I grabbed my phone off the bedside table and turned off the alarm three minutes before it was set to buzz me awake. Thoughts had been racing through my mind all night, and I'd barely slept. Peter looked equally bleary-eyed and said he hadn't slept either. We made coffee and were in the car half an hour later. At 3:55 a.m., we pulled into the meadow, where half a dozen people were milling about. We were parked across the street from Alex's van. The light was on, and I could see him through the windshield in his orange jacket, doing something at the kitchen counter. Alex had slept soundly, as usual. He exited the van, followed by a single camera guy who emerged from the shadows.

We let them get a little ways ahead, then Peter and I fell in behind. The moon was almost full and so bright we didn't need our headlamps. The ponderosa pines lining the trail cast moon shadows that we ducked in and out of like forest sprites. We were so stealthy that we startled a family of deer, which ran off into the woods. I felt like I did when I was a kid and I'd wait until my parents fell asleep so that I could climb out of my window and cause mayhem in the neighborhood with my Wiffle bat.

We found a log and sat down to wait about a hundred yards from the start of the route. Alex's headlight flickered through a thick scrub oak that stood between us and the spot where he was getting ready. He was putting on his shoes, cinching his chalk bag, and taking one last glug of water. He couldn't carry anything on his back, so instead he'd stashed some water and energy bars in a few spots along the route. Every once in a while, the bottom of the wall would light up when Alex panned it with his headlamp. Things got quiet. Time stood still. Had he started up? I couldn't see his light, but the moon was so bright that perhaps he had decided to climb without his headlamp.

Two climbers carrying a big wall rack and ropes walked past, within ten feet, but they didn't see us on the log. Peter and I said nothing. I was starting to wonder what was taking so long when Pablo Durana, one of the cameramen, emerged from the shadows. He had his headlamp off and was carrying a large camera in one hand. "Pssst." He looked up, surprised to find us sitting a few feet away.

"Hey," he said.

"What took him so long to get going?" I asked.

"He had to run off and take a nervous poo."

"How did he seem?"

"Casual. Just like normal. He was chatty, asking me how I was doing, stuff like that. Hey, I gotta run." As soon as he moved off, Alex's light appeared above the canopy, like a tiny ship setting forth from shore into a vertical ocean of rock.

CHAPTER TWENTY-FOUR
Distractions

Alex dipped his right hand into his chalk bag, gave it a shake to make sure his hands were well coated, then sunk his thick fingers into the fissure with his thumb facing down. The rock felt like he thought it would, a little cold, but not frigid. The cold was never an issue for his fingers, but already he could tell that his toes felt squeezed. This was one of the problems that he couldn't seem to find a way around. If he chose a bigger pair of shoes, his feet would be more comfortable right now, but by the time he got to the Boulder Problem, they would probably feel sloppy. So he went with the smaller 41s. But the footwork-intensive slab cruxes on the Freeblast would still be cold. It was essential that his shoes perform well on these moves. His right shoe felt especially constricting. No wonder—his ankle was still swollen and his Achilles tendon felt stiff, its flexibility restricted from being bound within the bruised muscles of his ankle for more than a month.

The crack flared slightly, but the size, which varied from half an inch to about an inch and a quarter, fit Alex's fingers like a glove. The jams were so secure that Alex knew both his feet could slip at the same time and he'd easily be able to check the fall. The flared crack made for secure foot jams too. With his toes twisted into the same pods he used for his finger jams, the chance for a foot slip, even if his toes were slightly numb, was nil. The only problem was that the climbing was so easy, he couldn't yet tell how he was feeling. Was this a day like the one he had on University Wall, when he had power to waste? Or would today feel more like Les Rivières Pourpres, more like work? It was too soon to tell.

It took less than a minute for Alex to enter the death zone. Once you're a hundred feet above the ground, you might as well be a thousand—the fall will be equally fatal. There's a rule of thumb climbers use to calculate the odds of dying in a ground fall. Fall ten feet and hit the ground and the chance of it being fatal is 10 percent. At twenty feet, 20 percent. From thirty feet up, you'll hit the ground at thirty miles per hour. This would be like riding a bike at full speed into a brick wall. The equation is straightforward—the higher you get (at least up to a point), the harder you hit that wall.

Alex reached the top of the second pitch, a 5.8 hand crack, seven minutes after leaving the ground. The third pitch starts with a rightward traverse under a roof. The climbing is thin and delicate and culminates with a move where everything depends on your foot holding on to a chip of rock the size of a quarter. Even though he was already two hundred feet up, the roof marked the real "game on" point. Alex threw his foot onto the tiny hold. Before committing, he double-checked with his headlamp to make sure it was placed precisely where he wanted it. Since he wasn't warmed up, it was critically important that he execute the move precisely according to plan. He was less worried about moves higher on the wall because by then he'd be in the flow and would be able to trust himself to do the right thing instinctively. Alex bore down on a crimp with his left hand, crushing the hold as if he were climbing 5.14. The right foot held, and he reached through to an incut edge with his right hand. Stepping through to better holds, he exhaled and panned his light up the wall. Off to his right he heard voices. He had seen that a party was starting up the Nose at more or less the exact time he was beginning his quest up Freerider. The pair was yelling back and forth noisily, no doubt communicating about taking in and letting out rope. A bulge in the cliff hid Alex's light from them, and so they had no idea what was happening 150 feet away.

The next two hundred feet involved straightforward finger jamming up discontinuous low-angle cracks. At the top of pitch four, four hundred feet above the ground, Alex stopped to rest at a small stance. Above him rose the first of the back-to-back crux slab pitches. This wasn't the one he had fallen on earlier in the season, but it was probably a little harder than that pitch. Alex stood on the tiny shelf and looked down at his feet. He wiggled his toes. *How do they feel?* he asked himself. *A little cold and numb.* He could stop and take off his shoes, rub his toes, but that would be dicey, and it would totally kill the flow he was trying to get into.

He looked down between his legs and saw two tiny lights at the base. Mark and Peter on their iPhones?

Alex looked up. At the top of the wall a beacon of light appeared, brighter than any headlamp he had ever seen. It had to be Mikey, who had surely spent a long, sleepless night on top. Everyone on the film crew knew that the money shot would be the Boulder Problem. It was thin, hard, unforgiving, and—at 2,100 feet above the valley floor—it could be framed from above in a way that would reveal the true grandeur and impossibility of what Alex was doing. And since Jimmy trusted Mikey more than anyone, they'd decided long ago that Mikey would get this shot. It would be hours before Alex got to the Boulder Problem, but Mikey was leaving nothing to chance. When Alex arrived, Mikey would be ready. The rope would be rigged exactly where he wanted it, the anchors bombproof, his stance locked down, camera angles dialed in, batteries charged, spare lenses at the ready.

There have been times when Alex has asked Mikey to film him soloing something and Mikey has said no. "Just go do it for yourself," he would say.

"It wasn't an easy decision to take this job," Mikey told me in Morocco. "Ultimately, I said yes because Alex truly wants me up there. And I do think I'm safer than a lot of other people. There are times when I'm five feet away from him filming, and if I slipped, I would kill him."

Alex shined his light on the crack splitting the wall in front of him, and located a small pod. He tucked the tips of his index and middle fingers on his right hand into the slot and twisted them to the right, pulling his elbow down toward the side of his chest. He tucked his right toe into a flare in the crack and reached high with his left hand to another pod. Years ago, before anyone had climbed this route, the crack was barely an eighth of an inch wide at its fattest, too small to fit anyone's fingers. To create a protection point, the first ascensionist nailed the thinnest piton, called a knife blade, into the crack. It bottomed out two inches in, half of its length sticking out. When his partner followed the pitch, he used his own hammer to knock the piton out, which meant banging it back and forth. In the process, the edges of the crack broke a little bit. After a few more ascents, the hole was big enough for the next size piton, and then after a few more, the next size. This process continued until the early 1970s, when climbers realized that something had to be done about the scarring that was changing the face of Yosemite's cliffs, and this began the "clean climbing revolution." The clean ethic relied on a new mode of protection called the "nut." The first nuts were exactly that—nuts from the hardware store or scrounged from alongside railroad tracks. Climbers slotted these rudimentary chocks, slung with webbing, into constrictions in the cracks with their fingers, not a hammer, and with them they could now climb a route a thousand times without ever leaving a trace of their passage.

A good many of the free climbs in Yosemite, including this section of Freerider, are only possible (at anywhere near their current rating) because of the artificial piton scars left behind as permanent reminders of the golden age. We love to celebrate the purity of our sport—communing with nature, living life on its simplest terms—but the truth is that it's all based on a haphazard short history full of human error and compromise.

Alex stepped over a small roof, where the crack petered out into a blank face. From here the route moves up and right past several bolts to the belay anchor about twenty feet above. He balanced on the last decent foothold before the first slab crux. The next move was unlike anything he had ever climbed without a rope—the "walking up glass" moves, as Alex had described them. At that moment, he would have gladly increased the difficulty rating in exchange for some holds. In Morocco, on Les Rivières Pourpres, he could overpower the moves because he had something to grip, but here, on the glacier-polished Yosemite granite, it was all about finesse.

The hardest moves *ever* climbed without a rope are three full number grades harder than this slab. In 2008, one of Britain's top rock climbers, Dave MacLeod, free soloed a route called Darwin Dixit in Spain—rated 5.14b. The route is only fifty feet high, but it overhangs a paved road. MacLeod wrote that "a fall from the technical or redpoint crux means the worst consequences," i.e., death. Before MacLeod's ascent of Darwin Dixit, the hardest free solo was an Austrian sport climb called Kommunist, rated 5.14a, climbed by the German Alexander Huber in 2004. The crux is approximately thirty-three feet above the ground, but Huber intentionally avoided using bouldering crash pads that could have softened a potential fall. In an interview afterward he said, "I worked on the route until the moment I could perfectly control it under good conditions. I was convinced I wouldn't fall, but like anything in life, you never know 100 percent. This sliver of potential danger is the essence of alpinism and climbing." Of course, thirty feet off the deck there is also more than a sliver of hope that you won't die if you fall. Alex, on the other hand, was now six hundred feet above the valley floor. It was 4:54 a.m. and still pitch-black. He felt his own sliver of doubt, but not about what would happen if he slipped.

Alex shined his light down by his right knee onto the spot where he knew he had to put his right foot. The day before, when he came down from climbing this section by headlamp with his friend Brad Gobright, he'd told a few people hanging outside his van, "Sometimes that kind of slab stuff is better in the dark because the shadows make the holds look bigger." This might be true if there's a bona fide imperfection in the rock, but the spot that now lay in the center of the yellowish halo cast by his headlamp had nothing to recommend it. There was no ripple, no depression in the rock; it was smooth, like a piece of gray construction paper. The reason it was the spot was not because there was something there to stand on. It was simply that it was in the right place, roughly in the zone where it would be possible to get over the right foot without having to hike his leg up too far. If he stepped too high, the weight transfer onto the smear would create too much downward pressure on his foot, which could cause it to slide out. What he needed right now was to use his body to push his foot *in* against the wall.

Alex has climbed more at night than most climbers have during the day, but nevertheless, it is still more difficult. Regardless of how well you can or can't see the holds among the shadows cast by your body and the myriad features of the rock, anyone who has climbed at night can attest that it *feels* different to climb in the dark, just like it feels different to hike in the dark. Perhaps it's our primal fear of what we can't see, of what might be lurking out there beyond the blinding glare of the campfire.

As he scanned the wall, Alex's light glinted off the bolt situated about a foot to the right of his knee. But rather than providing security, as it had on the thousands of ascents the Freeblast has seen over the years, it now lurked with a tinge of menace in its conspicuous attachment to nothing. Alex looked up. Fifty feet above and to his left, Matt Irving, a new recruit to Jimmy's team, hung on a fixed rope, his camera trained on Alex. Matt saw Alex staring at him. It was an awkward moment. Neither of them said anything—not yet. Alex was trying to get himself in the proper headspace to make this move, but it was just like Peter Croft had said. The camera guys, the journalists at the base of the cliff—it was all a bit distracting.

CHAPTER TWENTY-FIVE
Just Not My Day

"ROCK!!" A loud cracking sound filled the air—boulders tumbling downhill. My heart fluttered, but I quickly realized it was coming from farther up the west face. I checked my phone. It was 4:54. Alex had been climbing for about thirty minutes and appeared to have stopped on a small ledge. I assumed it was the stance at the top of pitch four. Peter, sitting beside me, was texting with editors back in Washington, DC, who were adding in the details he was supplying to the Google doc. Alex looked down, and his light shined on our hideout on the log. But instead of panning past, his headlamp stayed on us. Since we could see him, I guessed he could see us. "Hey, put your phone down," I said to Peter. "I think he's looking at us." *God, I hope we're not distracting him.* He stayed in the same spot for a few minutes, which I thought was odd. He wouldn't be tired yet, so why would he stop just when he was getting started?

I wondered if he was contemplating his chances. In Morocco, after he soloed Les Rivières Pourpres, we discussed the probabilities. He said he wanted—needed—his odds to be at least 99 percent. But he recognized that somewhere in the 90th percentile might be more realistic. Anything less than 99 percent was not what he called "repeatable," but Alex wondered aloud at one point if sometimes you just have to throw down all your chips and take the chance. I can remember learning, in my high school statistics class, about the exponential nature of probability. If there's a 99 percent chance that Alex won't fall on a difficult free solo, and he exposes himself to these odds a hundred times, the probability that he will survive to share these tales with his grandkids is .99 multiplied by itself a hundred times: 0.99^{100} comes out to .366, or 36.6 percent. Flipped around, that's a nearly two-thirds chance of a bad outcome. This is a gross oversimplification, especially because Alex is probably several .9s past 99 percent on most of his solos. But the math does reveal an indisputable truth about risk: keep on taking the risk, and the risk becomes greater.

Alex started moving again, but it was hard to see where he was exactly relative to the two slab cruxes. Voices drifted down from above. I looked at Peter, but he was absorbed in his note-taking. *That's odd*, I thought, keeping the idea to myself. *Why would Alex be talking to the cameraman?*

Alex's headlight lit up the bottom edge of the Half Dollar, but this time I could tell by how bright it was that he was in the crack system leading up to the flake. "He's done it," I whispered to Peter, gleefully rubbing my hands together. I sighed deeply. The tension that had been tying my stomach into knots over the last few days had untwisted a little bit. Alex had thousands of feet of rock ahead of him, including a number of 5.12 pitches and one pitch of 5.13a, but at that moment I believed he had the climb in the bag. "He's in cruiser territory for a while now," I said. "The sun will be up soon, so let's relocate to the meadow and get the spotting scope set up." It was 5:37 a.m.

As we packed up, Alex's light disappeared. I assumed he was somewhere up on Mammoth Terraces, a massive ledge system that marks the spot, a third of the way up El Capitan, where the lower slabs rear back into a two-thousand-foot vertical and overhanging headwall. I heard a noise and turned around to see Pablo, headlamp on, hustling up the trail.

"Hey, what's going on?" I called over as he scurried past, breathing hard. I had not expected to see him back up here.

"Alex is bailing," said Pablo. "He's on his way down."

"What? Why?"

"I don't know."

Peter and I were pulling out of the parking lot when Alex walked up. We must have seen Pablo seconds before he touched down. Alex saw us and looked over questioningly. I wanted to check in with him, but they were still filming and I wanted to respect his space, so I put the car in drive and did a U-turn. As we drove away, I saw Alex through the rearview mirror. He was looking in our direction, a frown on his face.

At 10:50 a.m., I was sipping coffee in the cafeteria with Peter Gwin and Peter Croft when a text came in from Alex. Sorry about this morning. Let's hang tonight. It made me a little sad that Alex was apologizing for bailing. He was feeling beholden. That wasn't right.

I texted back: I was proud when I heard you were coming down. U r the man. Yeah, let's hang tonight. Let me know what you guys end up doing.

I showed the text to the two Peters. Croft grimaced but didn't say anything. He had gone home a couple days earlier after accompanying Alex on one of his training sessions on the Freeblast. I had called him the night before to tell him that Alex was going for it. Croft left his home in Bishop on the east side of the Sierras at four a.m. to be here in time to witness Alex's historic climb. Croft said he had just come from Mike Gauthier's and that Alex had "freaked out."

"Suddenly he jumped on his bike and rode away. He said he needed to clear his head and that he was going to free solo Astroman." Alex must have texted me somewhere along the way to Washington Column, the formation on the eastern end of the valley where Astroman is located.

Gwin and I headed off to do some climbing of our own. When we got back to the ground, there was a text inviting us to dinner at the production house in Foresta.

We arrived a bit late. A dozen or so people were seated around a big dining room table. I grabbed a plate of food and found a seat next to Alex.

"Hey, I tried to come over and talk to you guys this morning," he said, "but you just drove away."

"Yeah, sorry about that. I thought you might want some space, so we just peaced out. How did it go up there?"

"I didn't feel that great. My shoes were too tight, and my toes were a little numb. It felt scary. I got to the move where I have to rock over onto that sketchy foot, and I knew if it blew that I was going to die. If I had been on my own I probably would have downclimbed to the nearest stance and tried to pull it together, but it just felt weird with the camera right there and all the people watching me."

"I'm so glad you made that call, dude," I said to Alex. I realized that it came off a bit patronizing, but I was genuinely impressed he had not bowed to the pressure. I was also a little worried he might be feeling guilty or remorseful for failing to come through with the performance the film-makers needed to cap off almost a year of production. After all, he had texted me earlier to say he was sorry. I wanted him to know that I thought it probably took more courage to back down than to push through.

"Yeah, it just wasn't my day, you know?" he said. And this was the genius of Alex. This is what many don't understand when they see some phenom do something they deem unthinkable, like climbing a cliff with no rope. Aside from the years of discipline, hard work, training, and studying every inch of the route, Alex also knew when he "had it" and when he didn't. In climbing, some days your feet might be there, but not your mind. Other days, you could be mentally prepared, but your body is fatigued or injured and can't pull it off. Alex was having a day where there were pieces missing from the puzzle, and he recognized it for what it was and bailed. He wouldn't have known this to be the case if he hadn't tried, and it was just one more stepping-stone to ultimately achieving his goal, as many "failures" often are.

CHAPTER TWENTY-SIX
The Conundrum

My conversation with Alex reminded me of what happened to Henry Barber in 1976 when a film crew talked him into on-sight soloing a 5.10 hand and finger crack on a sea cliff in Wales. Barber consented only on the condition that the cameramen were ready at the appointed time and that they didn't speak to him or distract him in any way while he was climbing. They agreed, but when the time came, the director told Barber to wait because the light wasn't right. Barber was tense and annoyed, and the cliff was blazing in the afternoon sun when they finally told him he could climb—four hours later. A few moves off the ground, a cameraman asked him to climb back down and start over.

"I started to climb and it seemed that everything was working against me," recounts Barber in his biography. "I felt the cameras and all of America watching me. . . . I just kept thinking, *Man, this is not where I want to be.*"

The climb quickly turned into a desperate battle. After lay-backing through the crux sixty feet up, Barber realized he couldn't reverse the moves he had just done and, worse, that he no longer had the heart for what he was doing. In the film, which aired on ABC's *American Sportsman*, you can see Barber shudder as he tries for a move, then backs off, realizing he doesn't have it. He looks tight. His characteristic flow on the rock is gone.

A friend of Barber's who was at the base of the cliff became so unnerved that she had to leave. He considered calling for one of the cameramen to drop him a rope, but he knew that if he did, it would ruin the film. *Why am I doing this?* Barber asked himself. *Is this for my ego, or so someone can make a successful film, or am I doing this for myself?*

When he finally topped out into a grassy meadow an hour and half after setting off, a different cameraman asked him to climb back down so he could film him topping out a second time. Barber agreed, but he now had tears in his eyes. When they finally turned off the cameras, he took off his shoes and threw them as far as he could. "I was beaten," he recounts in his book. "I wouldn't do anything like it again."

Different time, different circumstances. Same conundrum. With the inherent pressure to make a good film, how does a free soloist venture right up to the boundary of his limits when there is zero margin for over-confidence? When I was Alex's age, we called it "Kodak courage"—the tendency for people to push beyond their limits when performing for the camera. Nowadays, in a world where fatal wingsuit accidents are captured by blinking, helmet-mounted GoPros, we might more aptly call it "GoPro bravado." Even more insidious is the way social media has made it possible for people to feel the pressure to perform even when they're alone. "Engaging in risky behavior so that others will notice us is not a new concept that has only emerged with this generation," says Jerry Isaak, an associate professor of expeditionary studies at SUNY Plattsburgh. "What is new, however, is the nearly constant 'virtual presence' of the others we are trying to impress. With the development of social media and related technology, 'other people nearby' has been simultaneously expanded to a potentially worldwide audience and shrunk to the size and portability of a smartphone."

Some people thrive under the pressure of knowing their every move is being recorded for posterity, but there are others—and I think Alex Honnold and Henry Barber are in this category—who don't feel comfortable performing in front of a camera, at least not when they're operating near their limit. In these situations, rather than fomenting bravado, the camera creates feelings of stress and anxiety.

In 2014, while filming a commercial with Jimmy Chin in Yosemite, Alex was on his second solo lap on Heaven, the route Dean Potter first soloed in 2006. (In 2011, Alex had one-upped Dean Potter again, by "flashing" the route free solo, accomplishing it on his first try.) A few feet below the top, Alex made a long reach with his right hand and tried to push into a fist jam. But he couldn't quite find the sweet spot, so he dropped back to the sloping shelf, where he dangled by his outstretched arms thousands of feet above the valley floor. Three more times he tried the move, each time coming up a little shorter. My old friend Rob Frost was assisting Jimmy that day, and he says he could see Alex battling to hold it together. A few seconds later, Alex called for a rope. Jimmy and Rob were too far away to assist, but luckily there were two other cameramen operating a crane a few feet above Alex. They lowered him a line, and Alex used it to pull himself over the lip. He would later admit sheepishly that technically he had been rescued, but he was quick to qualify it, saying that if he had been alone he would have just chalked up a bunch and gone for it—and he's confident he would have stuck it. He also says he wouldn't have found himself in that position to begin with if he hadn't been performing for the cameras.

Snapping back to the present, I turned to Alex at the dinner table, "What about Astroman—how did that go?"

"I haven't been on it in seven years, and it felt hard," he said. "I almost fell on the Boulder Problem."

"What? You seriously almost fell?"

"Yeah. I got three moves in and my foot slipped, and I kind of sketched. So I downclimbed to the ledge, regrouped, and then I went for it. The move getting into the Harding Slot was really hard. I was like, 'Oh boy, it's game on.' I did the route in 1:13, which was probably the speed record."

I looked around to see if anyone else was listening. They weren't. I had the feeling Alex hadn't told anyone else about this close call. The Boulder Problem (not to be confused with the section of the same name on Freerider) is the technical crux of Astroman, a very thin crack at the start of pitch three. It's rated 5.11c, a grade and a half easier than the Boulder Problem on Freerider. A fall on either would mean the same thing. The only difference is how long you'd be in the air before the lights went out.

After dinner Croft, Gwin, and I headed back to my cabin. We opened a bottle of wine Croft had in his milk crate of provisions, and the three of us slumped on the couch.

"Did Alex tell you he almost fell on the Boulder Problem?" I asked Croft.

"No," he said, "I'm really sorry to hear that. I would love to hear him say he was rock-solid. The hardest stuff I've done, I just felt locked in. But you know, it's not that surprising. . . . [After the aborted attempt] he honestly looked like a caged animal. This whole movie thing just doesn't add up in terms of putting Alex in the proper headspace to get this done. It's like one plus one equals three."

A few days later it was time for me to leave the park and return home. I was on the road by five a.m., en route to Reno, where I planned to catch a flight back to the East Coast. On my way out of Foresta, I stopped at the dumpsters to drop off my trash. The temperature was below freezing. A brisk wind gave the air a bite I felt on the end of my nose. The sky was filled with twinkling stars, reminding me of the night one week ago when Alex had set off up Freerider. For some reason, the nip in the air brought me back to some of the inhospitable places climbing had taken me over the years. Type-two fun, as someone had once described it—god-awful while it's happening, sublime when it's over. In a strange way, it felt like that to be heading home. A sense of relief that it was over, that Alex was still alive, but also a tinge of disappointment. A part of me didn't want to return to the humdrum of normal everyday life. Despite the stress of witnessing Alex's climbs, I was enjoying being in the park again, reliving my days as a full-time climber when I was younger.

When my plane took off, Alex was sitting in El Cap Meadow, staring up at Freerider with one of his black books in his lap, reminding himself of everything he had learned about the route over the past two months—the tiny ripple on pitch five that gave him something to balance his hand on while he rocked over the sketchy foot; the way the karate kick at the end of the Boulder Problem felt slightly better when he sagged his hips before throwing it; the importance of getting the perfect pair of shoes—not too tight and not too loose. But most of all, he thought about how there weren't any showstopper moves. His dream was doable.

It just had to be the right day.

CHAPTER TWENTY-SEVEN
Fun

It was the last week in May of 2017, six months after Alex's first attempt at soloing El Capitan, and the spring climbing season was well underway. I was back in Yosemite in anticipation of Alex's second attempt of Freerider because the conditions for it were right. His determination to make it happen had not wavered. He had been setting himself up for this grand mission for over a decade, and one failed attempt was simply another stepping-stone in the process. It was an unplanned hiccup, but Alex's new knowledge of the climb would prepare him for another go at it.

We were having a mellow evening in his van, discussing some of our usual topics. It was hot and stuffy, but Alex didn't seem bothered. He sat sideways in the rear-facing passenger seat, his left leg propped on the driver's side seatback. His size 12.5 foot hung in the air, toes splayed, like a giant eagle talon. Considering the millions of feet of rock that he's climbed in his life, and that his go-to climbing shoe size is 8.5, his toes appeared surprisingly un-gnarled—apart from a grape-sized corn on his big toe.

I perched on his bed, feet dangling above the floor, admiring some photos pinned high on the wall above the galley. One of them was a shot I recognized from one of our expeditions together, a silhouette of Alex clinging to a wall high above the Gulf of Oman as the sun set over the Musandam Peninsula.

A college-ruled composition book with a geometric pattern of black and white triangles on its cover sat on the countertop to my left. A random name—Cody Quakenbush—was handwritten on its front. I later found out that Cody was a student of Alex's mom at American River College. I wondered if Cody knew that Alex Honnold was using his notebook for his list of things to do before free soloing El Capitan.

"There's no ventilation in here, huh?" I said.

"Naw," said Alex. "If I open the door or a window the van will get filled with mosquitoes, and they'll keep me up all night buzzing around my head. That's a total rookie maneuver."

The door was sealed tight, and the windows were filled with pieces of foil-backed foam. It was dusk, and hardly any light leaked in through the cracks. I could see why Alex called it "the box." The air felt heavy.

I hadn't seen Alex since November when we parted ways at the Cookie Cliff. Over the winter, we had spoken a few times by phone.

His plans for the spring sounded like they were up in the air. Of course, he planned to head back to the valley, but he didn't sound 100 percent committed to the project. Then he mentioned, casually, that he might just go and solo Freerider on his own—without the camera crew. As predicted, he had been thinking a lot about his aborted attempt. "I don't really mind having somebody around if I think the climbing's all easy and I'm just charging," he would later tell me. "But I never really want people around when it's actually hard." Freerider was actually hard, to say the least.

"I erased all my social media. I don't want the distraction in these final days, and I'm a little worried about what all the scrolling on my phone might be doing to my brain. I'm kind of nostalgic for the old days before I had a smartphone. I used to do a lot of quality thinking in the box back then."

I had similar concerns. To limit how much internet I consumed each day, I had been playing recently with an IQ app. Alex's eyes opened wide when I told him about it. He sat up straight, grabbed his iPhone, and pulled up the app store. "Which one did you download?" he asked, scrolling down the list and reading the names off to me. "What are the questions like?"

"Scrambled words, detecting patterns, math problems, stuff like that. It's a good way to use parts of your brain that might not see a lot of action, since you probably don't spend much time thinking in those ways. I know you did a lot of math and science when you were a kid, so think about how much of your brain is sitting unused nowadays."

"It's funny you mention that. I've actually been making a conscious effort to reassign all the neural pathways I used to use for math for memorizing beta."

The "beta," or helpful instructions on how to climb Freerider, could fill a book.

"Is that what you think about when you shut yourself up in the box?"

"Yeah, pretty much."

"Does it ever get boring?"

"No way, I love it. I could sit in here for hours by myself and just get totally lost in my head."

We both sat quietly for a bit.

I stood up and made a move toward the door of the van. It was eight p.m., Alex's bedtime. And that's when he locked on to me with his big brown eyes and said, "I leave for Alaska on the twelfth [of June], so that will give me about eight days to get it done." I stared back at him, waiting for the qualifier, the "We'll see, we'll see" that he always tacked on whenever we talked about Freerider. But he just looked at me earnestly and said nothing more. And it struck me that this was probably yet another step in the process he had laid out for himself years ago—the part where he tells someone, without being explicit, that he's made a decision. He was going for it on or around June 3. And I knew that somewhere, maybe in the Cody Quakenbush notebook, he would have this written down—noted simply as "EC" (El Cap).

CHAPTER TWENTY-EIGHT
Climbing with Alex

Alex called one morning and said, "Hey, man, how's it going? I just soloed Easy Rider."

"How was it?" Easy Rider is the U-shaped linkup Dean Potter pioneered in 2011 that climbs the top six pitches of Freerider.

"It was soooo good," said Alex. "Uhh, we're breaking up, let me call you right back."

My phone rang a minute later. "Sorry about that. I jumped the gun. I know the phone doesn't work until I get to the tree at the top of the Nose, but I thought I'd try it a little early. I should be good now." I could hear scuffling and wind. He was on the move, hoofing down the summit slabs of El Cap. Always the multitasker, Alex usually calls someone when hiking down from El Cap. And he always times himself. Despite talking to me, he would set his record that day, making it from the top of Freerider to Mike's house in a little over an hour; a factoid Alex would scribe into his notebook that evening.

"Hey, so do you want to go up the Freeblast with me tomorrow?" he asked. I was worried. It had been a while since I had climbed El Cap, and I did not want to be responsible for anything bad happening to Alex on the wall. I hesitated for a few seconds, then I just blurted out the truth. "I do, but I'm really worried that I'm going to hold you back and that I could fall and pull you off."

"No way, don't worry," he said. "I have a plan. We'll use Mini Traxions and you'll be fine. And it will be fun to get up on the Captain together."

"Are you sure?"

"Totally."

At five forty-five a.m. the next morning I was standing at the base of El Cap with Alex. Jimmy and Cheyne Lempe were planning to do some filming and had already headed up some fixed ropes. Alex reached into his black vinyl-coated pack and pulled out a ratty orange-and-white-flecked rope. The sheath was covered in little nicks, the end had unraveled, and there were strands of white core sticking out messily.

"That's our rope?"

"Yeah, what's wrong with it?"

"It looks like it's been through a war."

"Whatever," said Alex, looking mildly annoyed. "This is actually the best rope I own. It's fine."

Alex had cut the bottom of the legs off the black nylon pants he always wore, turning them into capris. But instead of carefully marking where on the cuff he wanted to shorten them and using a pair of scissors to make a clean cut, it looked like he'd hacked them off with a sharp rock. The legs were different lengths, the new hemline festooned with tatty triangles of fabric. He looked like a Flintstones character.

"Solo up to that ledge and put me on belay up there," said Alex, pointing to a shelf of rock forty feet above our heads. I must have looked incredulous, because he then added, "It's only 5.7." Without waiting to hear whether I was comfortable starting our day with some free soloing, Alex took off. He was halfway up the first pitch when I got to the ledge. I pulled the rest of the rope up and tied into the end as it whipped off the shelf like pot warp reeling off the deck of a crab fishing boat. I barely had time to dip my hands into my chalk bag before the rope came tight on my harness. Time to move.

My job was to make sure the rope never tugged on my harness. Each time it did, it meant Alex couldn't move up. The guy is generally unflappable, but if you want to test his patience, try simul-climbing with him and continuously bringing him up short. Jimmy once likened Alex to a racehorse: "You can't hold him back once you let him out of the gate." In that same conversation, Jimmy also told me that Alex had "fired" him because he moved too slowly one day when they were simul-climbing on the Freeblast. I knew this was going to hurt, but I underestimated how much. I felt like I was at a track meet. One minute I was standing around waiting for my heat, the next I was going all out and looking for a secluded place to vomit behind the bleachers.

But there was something else I hadn't anticipated: how fun it would be. Alex was placing one or two pieces per pitch, so there was hardly anything for me to do besides climb. And while he had an anvil (me) hanging off his harness, I had the opposite: the rope pulling me up from above like some magic beanstalk. Moving so fast over so much stone, I wondered whether it's how a bird feels when it flies, or a monkey as it swings through the canopy—a joy so deeply rooted in your soul that it makes you feel like you're doing exactly what you're supposed to be doing. Tom Frost, one of the Salathé Wall's first ascensionists, described this feeling as a religious experience: "The whole route felt like the Creator made it just for traditional climbers who would feel the love and fall in love in return."

I couldn't see Alex, because a bulge in the rock was blocking my view of him, but I could see the mighty bulk of El Capitan hanging above me like some Gothic cathedral. Climbing, even on some little rock in the woods, is a joyful experience, but doing it on the side of a geologic marvel like El Capitan feels like a spiritual awakening. I felt like Stuart Little would if he walked into Notre Dame.

On the fifth pitch, the rope hung limply in front of me, which was not how I wanted it. I wanted it tight, like guitar-string tight, because at that moment, I wasn't sure how I was still stuck on. My toes were bent backward on the 70-degree rock, making a deep crease in the leather on the top of my shoe. My fingers were pressed against blank rock on either side of my shoulders. There was nothing to grip, but my skin must have been adhering to something, because I knew that if I let go with either hand, I would slip off.

By this point, Alex was belaying me from the anchor at the top of pitch six. I wondered if he was keeping the rope slack on purpose. He told me on the hike in that Jimmy was assuming I was going to fall and looking forward to it, because he had almost no footage of anyone flailing on Freerider. I knew Jimmy and Alex both worried that the footage would somehow fail to capture how difficult and tenuous the climbing is on this section and therefore what it really means to free solo El Capitan. I looked up and to the left. Jimmy was hanging on a fixed line, his camera trained right on me. He didn't say anything. If I was going to avoid being that guy who fell in his film, I needed to keep moving before my feet melted out from under me. I could feel them slowly oozing off the smears. But I already had a loop of slack in front of me, and if I moved up and Alex didn't reel it in, I could slide ten to fifteen feet before the rope would snap tight on my harness.

"Up rope," I finally yelled. A few seconds passed—nothing. A few more. At the exact moment the rope came tight, my left foot skated out from under me. My fingertips bent backward, but somehow I didn't slide off the wall. I took a few deep breaths to center myself, and then my left foot skated out from under me a second time. Again, I didn't fall, but I felt improbably adhered to the rock, as if I were cheating the laws of physics. At that moment I thought of myself in this position without a rope. My guts quivered.

Higher up, Alex directed me off right onto one of his variations that followed a series of small ledges cut like stairs into the rock. The staircase ended at a horizontal band of calcite thirty feet below the ledge where Alex was belaying. He coached me through the moves, which turned out to be even harder than the ones I'd just done. The handholds were on the left, footholds on the right, which forced me into an unfamiliar yoga-like contortion.

"Stick your left toe in the divot," said Alex. I looked out left and saw a triangle-shaped hole that looked like a snake eye. It was big enough for a pea-sized chunk of rubber on the front of my shoe. I rocked over it like it was a ledge, committing my entire weight to it, knowing I just had to trust it because there was no other way to do this move—which is fine when there's a guy thirty feet above holding your rope.

"Nice job," said Alex, when I met him at anchor. It had been close, but I hadn't fallen on any of the pitches.

"How'd it go for you?" I asked.

"I'm grumpy," he replied.

"How come? Because of me? Because I was so slow?"

"Kind of. You did fine, but I had to wait for you in the middle of the first crux, a place where you want to just quickly move through, and so I fell. I wanted it to feel easy and it wasn't. I'm going to head back down and check it out a little more."

"Do you want a belay?"

"No, I think it will be easier if I just self-belay with my GriGri."

Alex told me it was going to be hot on the wall, and it probably would be later in the day, but in the shade, with the stiff breeze, I was cold. I pulled up the hood on my shirt, and as I huddled on the ledge eating some jerky, I noticed an old bolt sticking out of the wall about five feet to the left of the main anchor. It was ancient, a rusted brownish blob with an iron ring fastened through the eye of its hanger. I assumed it was one of the original bolts from the first ascent in 1961. There aren't many of these old bolts in Yosemite anymore. Most of them have ripped out or have been replaced with beefy stainless steel bolts by the American Safe Climbing Association (ASCA). I used to own one, a memento of the fifty-foot fall I took when I ripped it out of the northwest face of Half Dome on my first big wall in 1990. The ASCA sometimes leaves an old one here and there as a historic relic. This particular one had quite a story to tell.

The Salathé Wall was the second route on El Capitan. The first ascensionists, Royal Robbins, Chuck Pratt, and Tom Frost, decided to up the ante on Warren Harding by climbing it in alpine style, which is when you carry with you everything you will need for the climb, from food to your shelter. Harding climbed El Capitan's first ascent, via the Nose route, in expedition style, which is when you set up fixed camps ahead of time. He spent a year and a half sieging the route with half-inch manila ropes and a wheeled cart for hauling supplies like coal in a mine. Robbins, Pratt, and Frost simply walked up to the base of the cliff and started up. I wondered if the ledge I was on was where they spent their first night. Perhaps they drilled the bolt so they had something secure to clip into as they bedded down right where I was sitting. What would they think about Alex climbing this wall fifty-six years later, without a rope? Frost was the only one still alive. Robbins had died in March. Pratt had died in 2000. When asked by *Outside* magazine which climbers he respected from the new generation, Robbins had called out Alex Honnold and Tommy Caldwell, saying, "Many of the things that are being done today were clearly impossible in our day. And they're doing them."

My mind wandered back to Alex and the fact that he'd just fallen again on the slab. In October, Alex told me that he'd climbed the Freeblast twenty or so times. And he'd fallen twice—10 percent of his attempts. I wasn't sure how many more times he had climbed it since, but even if he had doubled his previous tally, his ratio would be three out of forty: 7.5 percent. Sure, there were extenuating circumstances, like old codgers such as myself that forced him to stall out in the middle of the crux, shoes that were too loose or too tight, or just not being focused enough. But what struck me was that the odds seemed to have this weird way of staying consistent. The orange rope clipped to the anchor in front of me kept getting tight and then limp as Alex went up and down. He wasn't giving up. But this slab was getting into his head.

I realized then and there that he would never have this slab section dialed in to his satisfaction—no matter how many times he rehearsed the moves. And he must have known it too; the climbing was just too insecure for him to ever feel the degree of certainty he sought for free solos. I remembered the story he told me about the slab move at the top of Half Dome, how his subconscious mind simply would not allow him to make the move. The same thing had happened the previous fall in this same spot on his first attempt.

What would happen this time? I wondered. Alex had said this climb was so singularly special that it might be worth just saying "Whatever" and rolling the dice. The question was, could he override his instinct, which seemed to know, as only our primal selves can, that pulling this slab move without a rope was a very bad idea? Was Tommy right when he said that this whole business was just a game of Russian roulette?

"Well?" I asked when Alex pulled back onto the ledge.

"I'm just kind of bummed," he replied. "I was so excited that I had maybe found a way around the slabs, but these variations just aren't noticeably better. That move is really insecure. I don't like it."

We stood side by side for a minute or two.

"What do you want to do?" said Alex finally. "Do you want to keep going, or do you want to bail?"

"I'm easy," I replied. "I'm here to support you, so whatever you want to do is fine."

"I'm not really bothered to keep going," said Alex, "but I'm also not stoked to deal with all these people either." Looking down the wall, we could see two parties on their way up. We would have to rappel past them, and invariably, they would want to know what we were doing, if they didn't already know. For the past month, Alex had again been all over Freerider, working various sections on an almost daily basis. All the climbers in Yosemite, it seemed, were being respectful and discreet, but with each passing day, word of Alex's plan was spreading quickly. He didn't say so, but I suspected he bore extra psychological weight now that his secret was going viral. It all added up to a whole lot of people, most of whom Alex didn't know, having expectations of him.

CHAPTER TWENTY-NINE
Final Preparations

Toward the back of El Cap Meadow, there's an oak tree that sits on the bank of the Merced River. The trunk is about four or five feet across, which would make it about three hundred years old. Its dense canopy throws shade over the lush green grass, but in a couple of spots, where people like to sit, the grass is thinner and matted down. With your back against its trunk, you can take in the entirety of El Capitan, from the west face on its left side, around the Nose, and all the way up the southeast face to Horsetail Fall and the East Buttress. The tree has always been the place for people to sit and admire the grandeur of a magnificent cliff.

The river, pumping with spring runoff, had partially flooded the meadow, but I found a dry spot under the tree where I set up my spotting scope and then plopped down into my camp chair. Starting at the rim, I ran the scope down the wall until I found Alex and Cheyne hanging on the anchor above the Boulder Problem. When Alex left the valley in the fall, he had climbed the Boulder Problem, Freerider's technical crux, about fifteen times in a row without falling a single time. I knew he'd done it a few more times this spring, including the two times he had climbed the route top to bottom, and as far as I knew, he hadn't fallen on it yet.

You can try a climb a hundred times and fail on the same move a hundred times. But if you then succeed on that move once, you may be able to do it every time from then on. Why is that? And what caused the mental block that prevented you from doing it in the first place when clearly you were capable of sticking the move all along? On climbing moves that are at or near your limit, there's a hard-to-define spirit, a ferocity you must tap into when going for that next hold. Without that little extra bit of oomph, your fingers can hit the hold over and over but never latch. Sometimes, it can feel like you're coming up short intentionally. This is such a well-known phenomenon in climbing that we even have a term for it—punting.

But once you've proven to yourself that you can do a move or even an entire route, it's like a tiny door opens inside your mind, and the belief that you can do it, that you will succeed, creates a powerful positive visualization. Golfers are famous for using this technique with their putting. Visualize the ball rolling into the cup and there is a far better chance it will actually go in. The actor Jim Carrey tells the story of using positive visualization to find career success. In 1987, before he was famous, he wrote himself a check for $10 million and on the memo line wrote "for acting services rendered." The story goes that he carried it around in his wallet until he finally found his breakout role in 1994.

In a way, it's what Alex was doing on Freerider. All of the time he spent rehearsing the route was partly to memorize sequences and learn the intricacies of movement that would give him the greatest margin for error when executing the moves without a rope. But every time he succeeded on a crux move, he also added a few rings of chain mail to the mental armor he would wear when he set off on his ultimate climb.

I had to blink to make sure my eyes weren't deceiving me when I saw Alex swing off the rock near the top of the Boulder Problem. I wasn't watching closely enough to see which move he slipped on, but one second he was on the wall and the next he was dangling on the rope. He hung in his harness for a few seconds, then pulled back on and climbed up to the anchor. A few minutes later, he and Cheyne continued simul-rappelling down the wall.

As Alex neared the bottom of the cliff, I packed up my stuff and hiked to the base to meet him. I grabbed a tree branch to use as a walking stick on the hike up.

"You look like some kind of Boy Scout troop leader," said Alex, chuckling. "And hey, cool shirt, have you been to Mont-Saint-Michel?"

"I haven't. I got this from my son Will, who just did a French exchange program with his high school. He said it was his favorite spot in France. He brought me back this shirt and some special Mont-Saint-Michel salt that apparently they have in these sheds free for the taking."

"That's so funny," said Alex. "Because I can picture that. I was there as a kid, and I remember my parents buying me this little toy crossbow."

"How old were you?"

"Like four."

"And you remember it?"

"I do. Isn't that weird?"

And it was, kind of, because Alex had told me on other occasions that he remembers almost nothing from his childhood.

On the hike out, Alex stopped to look at his phone. I thought he was texting until he said, "Wow, Trump just pulled us out of the Paris Agreement.

That is so depressing." The news had just broken that minute. Alex looked dejected.

"You knew he was going to do it, didn't you?"

"I know they were saying so, but I was still hoping."

Alex doesn't talk much about his environmentalism, but it's one of his most deeply held convictions. Ted Hesser, the guy who shared his energy reports with Alex and now works for the Honnold Foundation, told me that Alex had recently written a $50,000 check to help jumpstart a grassroots solar power initiative in Ethiopia. This was the first I'd heard about it. If I hadn't gone climbing with Ted, I never would have known. There were no press releases, no posts on Alex's social media.

"So how'd it go up there?"

"It went well," said Alex. Either he had forgotten about falling on the Boulder Problem or he was choosing to put it out of his mind. "The route's in good shape. All my tick marks are still there, and it's totally dry. Conditions are pretty much perfect, and I think that's it. I don't think I'm going back up."

He sounded relieved to finally be done prepping the route, but the endless trips up and down El Cap over the past year had taken a toll on him physically. His eyes were glassy, and the crow's feet on their edges looked deeper than I remembered them. A few days earlier, while I sat in the passenger seat of his van as he did yet another hangboard session, he admitted that he was profoundly tired. "Every time I hike to the top of El Cap my legs just feel dead." He said he felt tired all winter and that there were many days when he wasn't happy with how he was climbing. But he did have one week of "total transcendence." All along, I had been wondering how he could time this so that he went for it on a day when he was feeling transcendent. For every athlete who has a personal best at the Olympics, there's a dozen more who don't peak right when they need to. But for Alex, there was more on the line than the chance to win an Olympic medal. What he was endeavoring to do would be like going for the world record long jump between two skyscrapers spaced twenty-nine and a half feet apart.

As we strolled down the trail, El Cap at our back, it hit home for me, perhaps more poignantly than it ever had before, that the guy in front of me was more like the rest of us than we like to admit. He gets migraines and has a wicked sweet tooth. Sometimes he feels like he's wearing lead shoes. Once in a while, though he doesn't want to admit it, he falls unexpectedly.

"How did the slabs feel?"

"Really insecure. I still always feel like my feet could slip. But at the same time, I'm like, 'Well, it's worked every time.'"

I didn't say what I was thinking. *Actually, it hadn't worked every time.*

When we walked into Mike's driveway, we saw a small blue hatchback parked next to Alex's van. "Oh wow, my mom's here," said Alex, who looked a bit taken aback.

We found her on the front porch eating lunch with two friends. Alex and I gave his mom a hug, and then she introduced us to her companions, who were visiting from France. Dierdre is tall and thin, and, like her son, she has distinctive-looking fingers. But they're not thick like Alex's. They're long and thin, with knobby knuckles. I remembered Alex once telling me that his mom is a lifelong piano player. I first met her in 2013 when she came to New Hampshire to do some rock climbing.

In November, a few days before Alex made his first attempt on Freerider, I went climbing with Dierdre. It was a bit surreal because she had no idea what her son was planning, and I didn't mention it. The night before our climb, she told me the story about the first and only time she had watched her son free solo. She and Alex were road tripping on the East Coast, on their way to a family reunion, when Alex, who was seventeen at the time, asked if they could stop in the Shawangunks, a popular climbing area in the Catskills outside New York City. They were hiking under a famous cliff called the Near Trapps when Alex disappeared. Dierdre looked up and down the trail, wondering where he could have gone. Then she finally looked up and saw him clinging to the side of a cliff overhead. "Get down here," she yelled. "I'm fine, Mom," replied Alex.

"How did that feel to watch him being up off the ground without a rope?" I asked Dierdre.

"Well, I had to force myself to trust his judgment, because I didn't have any judgment in this type of situation. I'm thinking, 'Well, he obviously knows what he's doing, let him do it.'"

In the years since that first solo, as Alex slowly developed into an unparalleled free soloist, Dierdre always heard about his climbs afterward. She meticulously collected clippings from newspapers, magazines, and the internet about her son's exploits. The scrapbooks, which Alex's friends call his Hall of Fame, can still be found to this day on the coffee table in her living room. What goes through a parent's mind, I wondered, when they hear that their child has just scaled a two-thousand-foot sheer cliff without a rope?

"A sigh of relief, you know, that kind of thing," Dierdre said. "And 'Wow! My son did that?' There's that side of it too. He's done these outstanding, outrageous things that nobody else can do. That's an honor, you know. But also, I wish he wouldn't."

I took a group photo of the four of them on Mike's porch. Diedre is a language professor who brought Alex up speaking only French at home. They were speaking in French after the photo, and while mine is rusty, it sounded like Dierdre was asking Alex if he would go on a hike with them. "Oui, oui," he replied. Alex didn't say anything about the big plans he had up his sleeve, and his mom didn't ask. But she did give me an inquisitive look as I bid them all adieu. A few days earlier, Jimmy had told me that Dierdre finally figured it out. She knew.

CHAPTER THIRTY
What Are the Odds?

Tommy Caldwell showed up over Memorial Day weekend for a quick visit. Alex seized the opportunity and dragged him up Freerider in five and a half hours, a new speed record for the route. "Alex was on fire," Tommy told me the next day, as we hiked up to the start of the Dawn Wall. He said that while he was up on Freerider he tried to imagine free soloing the route himself. "Honestly, I really can't fathom it."

"Did you guys talk about it?"

"I'm really hesitant to say anything at this point. Before, I was expressing a lot of doubt, telling him how I felt about it all. Now I'm a little bit more like, 'He's going to do it no matter what,' so the best thing I can do is try and up his chances of success. And for me that means trying not to mentally rattle him. I don't want him up there having doubts because other people are having doubts."

We found our way to a giant concavity in the southeast face called the Alcove. It marks the start of the Dawn Wall and several other famous routes like the Reticent Wall, Mescalito, and South Seas—I had set off from here on all of them. Tommy and I found a flat place to sit down with our backs to the cliff. The overhang of the Dawn Wall is so vast that we could see it rising in front of us. A portaledge covered in a red rain fly was hanging about 1,200 feet up.

"That's the camp where I spent months of my life," said Tommy. "The crux pitches are right above it." We could see one guy on the wall above the portaledge. The other one was probably belaying him from inside the ledge. They were aid-climbers and had already been on the wall for several days.

I asked Tommy how he was feeling about Alex's odds. "Do you think it's less than 1 percent that he will fall?"

"No way," he replied. "I think it's like 10 percent, if I had to put a number on it."

"That high?"

"Well, I know you've done the math. If he's done the Freeblast thirty times and fallen three, that's 10 percent right there. And it's not like that's the only hard, insecure climbing on the route. If I were to go free solo it right now, I would be way less worried about the slabs than some of the stuff up high. I've actually never fallen on the Freeblast, and I've climbed it fifteen to twenty times. But I've always felt real lucky to get through the Boulder Problem, and yesterday I fell on it. Alex was right above me, coaching me through the moves, but I missed when I threw the karate kick."

"Why do you think he's fallen on it as much as he has? Is he not a slab master?"

"Maybe not. Then again, I feel like Alex has climbed twice as much rock as anybody in the world . . . ever. Seems like maybe it's gotten in his head." He didn't say anything for a bit, then added, "I think I'm okay that I'm not going to be here. It's not really the kind of thing I want to spectate."

Tommy started to whistle. I wondered if he'd picked up the habit from Alex or vice versa. They're the only two guys I know who whistle.

▲▲

I had to move out the next day because the property that I was staying on in Foresta was hosting a music festival and the band was staying in my apartment. I called the reservations number for the park to see if by some miracle there were any campsites, tent cabins, or hotel rooms open, but of course there was nothing. It was Friday, June 2, and the park was thronged with tourists. I was planning to sleep in a cave and hope that I didn't get caught by a park ranger when my phone buzzed.

Looks like it is on. I'm headed up in an hour or so, said the text from Jimmy. Alex had gone bouldering that morning and then hiking in the afternoon with his mom and her friends. He told me he was going to take two full rest days before he went for the climb. And his mom was still in the valley. I assumed he wouldn't go for it until she left, because her presence carried a psychological weight—a weight that I didn't think he'd want on his shoulders when he set off. *Maybe he's just sick of waiting*, I thought.

One thing was sure: if I was going to be up early to watch Alex, I really didn't want to sleep under a rock. With my luck, I'd get caught and kicked out of the park. On a whim, I called a hotel in El Portal, just outside the park boundary. They'd had a cancellation and had a room available.

Half an hour later, I was parked at a pullout on the west side of El Cap Meadow, near the spot where I planned to watch the climb in the morning. I decided not to go straight to the hotel but rather have some time to myself in the park and allow the weight of the next day's events to sink in. I stood outside the driver's side with the door open. "If You Leave Me Now" by Chicago played on the car's radio as I watched the last rays of sun slowly creep up the west face of El Capitan. I traced the line of Freerider from where it appeared just above the trees and spotted a party of climbers on Mammoth Terraces setting up their portaledge for the night. On dozens of nights in portaledges on the side of El Cap, back against the wall, I've felt the heat from the stone radiating like a fireplace hearth. We used to drag along a boom box, which we padded with duct tape and foam from an old blown-out sleeping pad. All day long we'd listen to 104.1—The Hawk—the same station I was listening to now. I wondered if people still did that, if maybe the folks up on Mammoth—the ones that were going to wake up to the equivalent of an alien sighting in the morning—were listening to Chicago right now.

I tried to picture Alex up on the wall, but my mind didn't want to go there. Instead, it kept conjuring up a different image. *Alex trots out of the woods near the base of the Manure Pile Buttress. His face is glowing. He comes over to where I'm waiting and gives me a hug.* I looked around; there was no one nearby. I leaned on my forearms. Tears dripped off my cheeks and puddled on the roof of the rental car.

CHAPTER THIRTY–ONE

It's Happening

When Alex woke up on June 3, 2017, it was pitch-black in the box. *Okay, let's do this.* But when he picked up his phone, he saw to his disappointment that it was still only two thirty a.m. He rolled over and fell right back asleep. Two hours later his alarm jolted him awake. He swung his legs off the edge of the bed and hopped down onto his feet. Once standing upright, he realized that he didn't feel so great. He had gone to bed with a headache, and it lingered. Might have been from watching *The Hobbit* the afternoon before. Watching movies during the day often gave him headaches. Or it could have been the many hours he spent speaking French on the hikes with his mom and her friends the past two days.

He flipped on the galley light, and his breakfast was sitting on the countertop, premade from the night before—a bowl of muesli topped with chia seeds, flax, and blueberries. He grabbed a carton of hemp milk from the mini fridge and poured it over the top, then sat in the passenger seat holding the bowl in his lap. The muesli was a stash that he had been saving for this morning. The past few days he had been eating a different variety sold in the Yosemite grocery store, and he didn't like it as much. So he went back to the brand he likes but was surprised when he lost his appetite halfway through the bowl—he usually devoured his breakfast. The banana, which he always ate after the muesli, sat untouched on the counter.

Alex slipped behind the wheel of the van and backed out slowly onto Lost Arrow Road. He took a right turn down Oak Lane, slowing as he crossed the two speed bumps outside the Yosemite school. A minute later he was rolling down the loop road toward El Capitan.

At the trailhead, it was still dark, so he threw on a headlamp. He carried a small black backpack with his shoes, a chalk bag, a water bottle, and a chocolate chip CLIF Kid Zbar. He wore a pair of tattered North Face approach shoes, his cut-off pants, a red T-shirt, and a thin fleece hoodie. Near the base of the cliff, he heard a commotion and saw a bear thrashing through the bushes toward the fixed lines coming down from the Nose. Alex looked up at the three-thousand-foot vertical wall above him. *That's a big cliff*, he said to himself. Then he sat down and slipped on his climbing shoes. A few minutes later, he fastened his chalk bag around his waist, teed up his favorite playlist of "gnarly hate rock" on his iPhone, found his first toehold, and began inching his way upward.

He was barely off the ground when he heard jangling in the woods. Two climbers emerged from under the trees and looked up the wall. There was a guy on the first pitch of the Freeblast wearing scrappy cut-off black pants and a red T-shirt. And he wasn't attached to a rope.

"Oh my god," said one of them. "It's happening."

At 5:35 a.m., a tiny dot appeared just above the forest. I plopped into my camp chair, feeling thankful for my puffy coat, hat, and gloves. According to the thermometer in the rental car, it was 58 degrees, but it felt colder sitting in the mist that had settled over the meadow. The tall grass was covered in dew, and my legs were soaked from the knees down. I pulled up my hood, tried to ignore the swarm of mosquitoes around my head, and looked for Alex through the eyepiece of my spotting scope. When I found him in the viewfinder, he was already 150 feet off the ground—well into the death zone. He was moving steadily upward, and I had to constantly adjust the angle of the spotting scope to keep him in the frame, which covered about a hundred feet of cliff.

There was a small red bundle on the back of his left hip—his hoodie, which he had rolled up and tied around his waist. I thought it was odd that he wouldn't either wear it or leave it behind. During the drive up from El Portal the sky had been gray, like it always is at dawn, but it had stayed that way. A high cloud blocked the sun.

Twelve minutes later, Alex hauled himself up onto a small pedestal at the top of pitch four. He reached down, unlaced his left shoe, and slipped the heel off the back of his foot, then did the same with his right. Above him rose the first of the crux slab pitches. The move that had caused him to abort in the fall was about fifty feet above him. Alex looked down and stared directly into the lens of the spotting scope. I doubt he could see me, but I could see him perfectly. I could see his eyes. They looked just like they always do, wide open. I grabbed my phone and texted this detail to Peter Gwin, who was back at National Geographic's headquarters in DC updating that same Google doc in real time as the climb unfolded.

Mikey Schaefer was standing next to me, wearing a blue cotton hoodie and filming with a large camera set on a tripod. He'd blown out his knee skiing a few weeks earlier and was getting surgery soon. He was walking with a limp, and there was no way he could work with the high-angle crew up on the wall.

After Alex's first attempt in the fall, and a lot of soul-searching, he decided not to have any camera guys on the crux pitches, so Mikey's long shot would be needed to document the entire climb. Jimmy and Alex had been discus-sing these details over the past few weeks, and they recently agreed that Jimmy and Cheyne would only film the top ten pitches of the route—the section that Alex had never fallen on. Of course, close-up footage of Alex on the slabs and the Boulder Problem was critical for the film, so they agreed on a compromise. Jimmy would capture these shots with remotely operated cameras that he would strap to the wall. For most of the climb, including all of the particularly difficult sections, the camera team would be invisible to Alex. Still, I wondered whether he could block out the virtual presence that was hovering in the ether all around him. Could he find the Zen that would allow him to enter that all-important flow state? He would have preferred that we weren't down here, or anywhere near El Cap, at all; he mentioned this to me a few different times—after his first attempt, over the winter, and then a week earlier when we were hanging out in his van. Even in the abstract, knowing we were watching his every move was a distraction.

Alex was caught in a classic catch-22. Filming this climb had been his idea, after all. And he still wanted the greatest achievement of his life to be captured for posterity. It was also a little late in the game to walk away and leave Jimmy hanging.

It felt like he stood on that ledge for half an hour, but when he pulled his shoes back on, I looked at my phone and only two minutes had elapsed. It was going to be a long morning. Alex set off, pulled over a small roof, and smeared his way up into the crux.

"I can't watch this," said Mikey, stepping away from his camera.

It was okay. He always felt this way at the beginning of a big solo. It took time to find the flow state, that old friend that allowed him to surrender, to trust that he was going to climb to the best of his ability. If he slipped? That was just the cost of doing business. On every other big solo, he compensated for the tightness by over-gripping. His fingers were so strong that he sometimes had to be careful he didn't rip the holds right off the mountain. And therein lay the problem he now faced: there were no handholds. He had no choice but to trust his feet.

But there was a tiny crust in the rock that he'd discovered in the fall. A crease no bigger than a perforation in a piece of notebook paper. It was a non-hold, almost like a tick mark—a thing that showed you where to put your hand. He was glad when he found it, because even if he couldn't actually hold on to it, it was comforting to know there was something underneath his fingers. And there it was, right in front of him. But he didn't put his hand there. Instead, he reached up and pinched his fingers through the shiny steel hanger, his forefinger touching the tip of his thumb as if he were making the okay sign. He was careful lest his fingers touch the metal. As long as he didn't grab the hanger, he reasoned, it wasn't cheating. Alex decided to make this compromise a few days earlier, after we climbed the slabs together and he lowered back down to do the moves again. He didn't mention it to me until we were hiking out. "I tried this new thing on the first slab crux on pitch five," he had said. "I pinched my finger through the hanger on that one sketchy foot move, the one I backed off on in the fall. I can do it without touching the hanger."

"Cool. Sort of like what you did on Half Dome with the carabiner, huh?"

"Yeah, exactly. I mean, if I fell I'm sure I'd break my finger."

"Well . . ."

"Yeah, it's a lot better than dying."

Alex looked up and felt thankful there was no cameraman dangling above him. This time he was alone.

He rocked up onto the horrible smear, his fingers hovering inside the hanger like he was playing the game Operation. He brought his left foot up, and for one or two seconds his body was splayed out, like a ski jumper doing a spread eagle. He shifted his weight onto his right foot, brought his left foot over to the same hold, and did a quick foot match. A second later he was through and onto good holds. The entire slab sequence had taken a total of twenty seconds. And for that brief moment in time, the equivalent of taking two deep breaths, there wasn't a person on the planet whose physical hold on the world was more tenuous. If he had so much as sneezed, it could have been the last move he ever made.

He quickly moved up through a swatch of vibrant lime green lichen and entered a serpentine band of calcite that stretched across the wall like a giant white snake. At the big step down on pitch six, he grabbed the good hold with his left hand, then switched it to his right. Leaning out to the left, he slowly lowered himself downward, his left foot tapping against the rock, all herky-jerky, as he dropped into a crouch and his right knee bent like a blade closing on a jackknife.

"That can't be fun," I said quietly. Mikey stood a few feet away, still with his back to the wall. Even from half a mile away, it was obvious Alex was feeling tight. But he had made it through. In three minutes, he had put both the slab cruxes behind him, moves that had haunted him for years. He scrambled onto the ledge above, sat down, and spent the next two minutes loosening the lacing on his shoes.

CHAPTER THIRTY-TWO
A Unicorn

About halfway up Freerider, there is a detached block stuck on the face of El Capitan known as the Hollow Flake, and it offers one of the more dangerous parts of the route. It's about a rope length long, with an off-width crack on its right side. The crack is roughly nine inches wide, which is an incredibly difficult margin to navigate because it's not big enough for a climber to fit inside it like a chimney, but it's so wide that it's very hard to place gear into it when climbers are trying to secure themselves via ropes. Even when a free climber arrives at the Hollow Flake, they often feel like they're soloing the pitch because there aren't many spots to place adequate protection.

The normal practice of climbing the Hollow Flake is to have your partner lower you while you pad sideways across a slab. It's called a tension traverse, and it's similar to a pendulum, except that you don't swing back and forth. Both techniques are common on big walls and used for moving across blank sections between crack systems. Mark Hudon and Max Jones, the first climbers to try free climbing this section of El Capitan (they managed to free climb all but three hundred feet of the route in 1979, an inspired effort), found a way to avoid the tension traverse with a difficult climb down a thin crack. Alex had always found the pitch especially difficult because his fingers don't fit in the crack, especially near the bottom.

Once, when climbing this pitch with Mason Earle, he had unexpectedly popped off.

Though free climbers don't like to admit it, it's easy to benefit from rope drag when traversing or downclimbing. If your partner is a little slow feeding the rope out, even a tiny bit of tension can prevent a slip.

It had famously happened to John Bachar on a route called Clever Lever in Colorado's Eldorado Canyon. Bachar had just climbed the route, which features a 5.12 lunge to a jug hold at the lip of a roof twenty feet above the ground. He felt so solid on it that when he got back to the ground, he decided to free solo it. At the crux, he threw for the jug and easily latched it. Unfortunately, he had failed to notice when doing it the first time that the weight of the rope running through the protection had checked his outward swing. Now, without a rope, his legs swung out so far from the wall that his body went horizontal and his hand slipped off the giant hold. He hit the ground feetfirst on the only flat spot in a garden of jagged boulders and then tumbled another ninety feet down a slab. When he came to a rest, he popped up to a sitting position and thought, *Wow, I'm okay*, a second before a boulder he had dislodged on his way down the hill slammed into his back, knocking him out cold.

On paper, the Monster Off-Width appears to be one of the easier pitches on Freerider. The topo shows a straight black line, and the grade is listed at 5.11a. But climbers familiar with this route know that the Monster got its name because it's been known to eat people alive. An "off-width" is the name for any crack that is too wide for standard jamming techniques. A slotted hand or a sideways clenched fist will usually jam well in a crack up

Alex Honnold in the Monster Off-Width during his free solo ascent of El Capitan on June 3, 2017.

to four inches wide. Any wider and you have to get creative with moves like hand stacks, arm bars, and chicken wings. The big difference between off-widths and regular cracks is that with an off-width you often can't hang off one arm while moving the other up, which means you have to lock yourself into the crack between moves with your legs. Off-width climbing is like trying to run up a steep hill wearing a heavy pack. The beta for the Monster on Mountain Project, an online guidebook, recommends carrying enough protection so you can build a mini anchor in the crack to hang off when you vomit from overexertion.

Alex was lucky because his size 12.5 foot, crammed into a size 8.5 shoe, fits perfectly when T-boned in the Monster. Climbers call this a heel-toe jam. Over and over, Alex pulled his right foot as high as he could, stuck it sideways in the crack, and then stood up on it while pulling himself up with a left-hand arm bar. His left hip, without a harness to get in the way, slid smoothly up the fissure. Like a snake, he methodically slithered his way up until his butt found a tiny shelf in the left wall the size of a toilet seat. Alex took in the view and thought about the Boulder Problem, which was now just a few hundred feet above him.

At 7:53 a.m., he scrambled into the alcove below El Cap Spire, a flat-topped 150-foot-tall tower that juts like an upturned thumb from the side of the wall. He'd made it just in time, because nature was calling. Behind the spire, he found an out-of-the-way spot and pooped into a crack. He felt awful about it and hoped it would rain—hard—before the next party came up it. But it had to happen, because he couldn't risk soiling his pants on the crux. Afterward, he hobbled around in the alcove with his pants around his ankles looking for rocks to use in lieu of toilet paper.

On a ledge below the Boulder Problem, Alex took off his shoes and shirt. For the second time of the day, he looked down directly into the lens of the spotting scope. Then he pulled down his pants, gave us what Mikey called "the full frontal," and took a leak. Afterward, he sat down and had a drink of water from a bottle he had previously stashed on the ledge. Seven minutes after he got there, he slipped his shoes and shirt back on, stood up, and shook his hands like a sprinter at the starting line of a hundred-meter dash. He slathered chalk onto the back of his hands and looked poised to set off when he sat back down and took his shoes off again.

"I can't watch this," said Mikey for the second time.

Minutes later, Alex had re-laced his shoes, a little more tightly this time, it appeared. He was now standing on the last good footholds below Freerider's crux. Unlike every other difficult patch on the route, these moves are so tenuous that there's only one way to do them. Other sections of the route, like the slabs, for example, have multiple possibilities. Alex could screw up a sequence there and still feel confident that he could get through the moves. On the Enduro Corner, there was a sequence for the jams—left-hand thumb up, right-hand thumb down—and he had ticked the holds accordingly. But he had also practiced the pitch "off-handed," as he called it, meaning he intentionally grabbed with the wrong hand. He told me that doing it this way didn't feel that much harder. There are thousands of individual moves on Freerider and, despite memorizing many of them, Alex trusted himself to figure a lot of them out on the fly. When he was in the flow state, his body sometimes knew what to do better than his mind did. This intuitive kinesthetic awareness that comes from years and years

Alex scales the Enduro Corner, 2,500 feet above the valley floor, on the first free solo of El Capitan on June 3, 2017. Tommy Caldwell called the feat "the first moon landing of free soloing."

of practice and discipline was how he found a lot of the refinements to his sequences. But the Boulder Problem isn't like that. As Alex had explained to me in exquisite detail that day in the van, there is one way—and one way only—to do it. And he knew that if he screwed it up, if he pushed his thumb against the pencil eraser hold in the wrong way, it would probably cause his feet to skate off the tiny nubs that were holding him up. And the handholds were so bad that if his foot slipped, there was no way he could check the fall.

After three hours of squinting with my left eye while I gazed through the scope with my right, I had developed a mild headache. I reached up to put my left hand over my eye, so I wouldn't have to scrunch it shut, and it felt wet on my face. My palms were sweating. The scope gave the illusion that I was watching Alex on a screen, like this was a YouTube video. But my pounding heart knew it was all too real. I must have looked away, because I don't now remember seeing him do the move. What I do remember is next seeing Alex's left leg stuck out horizontally like a dancer. He had nailed the karate kick—the 5.13a move, 2,100 feet in the air—that had spit him off two days earlier. A few seconds later, at 8:23 a.m., he pulled onto the ledge above the Boulder Problem, turned around, and held his hands over his head. It was a gesture somewhat out of character for Alex, but he was connecting with those of us who were witnessing the climb. He was sharing the joy.

CHAPTER THIRTY-THREE
Topping Out

The final pitches were like a victory lap. A warm breeze wafted up the wall. The valley floor, half a mile down, was spread like the tableau of a model train set. Old-growth black oak trees scattered across El Cap Meadow looked like pieces of broccoli, the vehicles inching along the loop road like Matchbox cars. The sun-stippled Merced River sparkled as it lazily flowed down the valley alongside the meadow that appeared to undulate as its tall golden grass swayed in the breeze.

This was the section of the climb that had been playing on the highlight reel in Alex's mind for the past nine years. By now he had spent so much time on Freerider that a lot of the holds felt like old friends. *I love this move,* he thought to himself, over and over, as he karate chopped his way up the perfect hand and finger cracks. As he joyfully reeled himself upward, he felt like the hero in an action movie of his own making—which, in a way, he was. A few feet away, Jimmy dangled on the end of a rope, camera trained on Alex.

There was no cheering crowd when Alex pulled over the final block, no spraying of champagne, no gushing reporters asking him what it felt like to have just completed the greatest rock climb of all time. Alex walked a few feet back from the edge and took off his shirt and shoes. He was covered in chalk from the tips of his fingers all the way up his Popeye-like forearms. He stood on the rim, squinting into the bright morning sun, arms by his side. It was 9:28 a.m. The first free solo ascent of El Capitan had taken three hours and fifty-six minutes.

Alex would later post a photo to Instagram of him and Jimmy hugging a few feet from the edge of the cliff. The caption reads: "I was elated, @jimmychin was probably just relieved that his movie had a happy ending." Jimmy's got both arms around Alex. His eyes are shut and his mouth is wide open, like he's yelling. Alex, standing erect and almost a head taller than Jimmy, wears an enigmatic, toothy smile.

My story breaking the news of Alex's historic ascent posted at ten a.m. It immediately went viral.

Tommy Caldwell had given me a quote. He called the climb "the moon landing of free soloing."

Peter Croft had said, "After this, I really don't see what's next. This is the big classic jump."

Later, *The New York Times* would write that Alex's free solo of El Capitan should be celebrated "as one of the great athletic feats of any kind, ever."

But there were haters too. The link to the story on National Geographic's Facebook page racked up over two thousand comments, and I was shocked at how many of them were negative.

Matt DuMont
PSA.
Free soloing anything is stupid.

Full stop.

Videoing it for posterity is negligent.

Caleb David

I never completely understand why people risk their lives for something so pointless. There are so many other ways to enjoy life . . .

Benjamin Holt

What Alex achieved is nothing short of amazing regarding the limits to which the human body can be trained. But comparing it to landing on the moon is nothing but a slap in the face to the thousands of individuals who made that possible . . .

There were also hundreds of comments from Alex's fans and supporters.

Mark Kittel

Gotta love all the Debbie Downers here, pissing on this guy's Wheaties just because they envy someone willing to take risks while they sit at home judging other people from the bottom of a bag of chips . . .

Alex never read any of them.

At 11:29 a.m. I heard a familiar whistle. A few seconds later, Alex emerged from the forest and trotted across the small meadow where I was waiting for him. The cropped pants were covered in chalk, as was his shirt. He wore a black baseball cap on his head, his ears sticking out from underneath. It felt a little odd as he jogged across the meadow and I stood there waiting. But the awkward moment only lasted a few seconds before Alex locked me in the warmest embrace I've ever had from him. I slapped him on the shoulder and then stepped back to take in his expression. He was glowing. I was too. This scene was playing out exactly how I had pictured it in my mind beforehand.

Alex sat down on a rock, and I dropped into the dirt next to him. It was hot. Mosquitoes buzzed around us. I looked down at his shoes. The laces, de-sheathed and broken, had been jury-rigged back together. Alex pulled an apple out of his pack and asked if I had any water. I gave him what was left in my bottle.

"So, did it go perfectly?" I asked.

"It went pretty much perfectly. I had to take a dump down behind the spire. I feel pretty bad about it. But it's just one of those things. I hope nobody's climbing Excalibur for a while. The idea of soloing the crux sort of loosened things up."

We sat a hundred yards off the trail to the Manure Pile Buttress. Climbers were walking back and forth, looking in our direction. By now, news outlets all over the world were reporting Alex's feat and climbers were reading about it on their phones. "Hey, Alex, glad you didn't die," yelled someone walking by on the trail.

I asked Alex if he had thought about anything other than the moves on his way up the climb. He said that on the easier sections, he was already thinking about his next goal, which was to climb the grade 9a (9a is a French grade, equivalent to 5.14d/5.15a on the Yosemite Decimal

System), two ticks below the world standard of 9c. It struck me as slightly preposterous that, having just made the greatest climb of all time, Alex would be looking forward to becoming the fiftieth-best sport climber in the world. But 9a happens to be one notch harder than what Alex has climbed to date. It's something that he will have to accomplish with the use of a rope, of course. But greater climbing prowess would open the door to more free solo projects as well. "Imagine what I could do if I were as strong as Adam Ondra," Alex had said one day between burns on the Beastmaker.

"So it's still just game on?" I asked.

"It's kind of been a strategy the whole time I've worked on this—to look past it, to think what's beyond, what other stuff I'm excited about. So this just feels like a semi-normal day. I want to eat some lunch, I want to get in the shade, and then I'm probably going to hangboard in a bit."

"A normal person would probably take the afternoon off after they free soloed El Cap," I replied.

"But I've been hangboarding every other day, and it's the other day."

An hour later, I was sitting on an upside-down canoe outside the door of Alex's van, which was now parked back in Mike's driveway. Birds chirped and flitted among the branches of the oak trees overhead. Yosemite Falls roared in the background, so ever-present it hardly registered. On Lost Arrow Road, there were no news trucks, no groupies, no rangers offering congratulations. It was just Alex and me.

So I sat there. And I watched Alex. Barefoot and bare-chested, wearing only a pair of bright red shorts, he hung two-handed from the Beastmaker. Because he had been hangboarding every other day. And today was the other day.

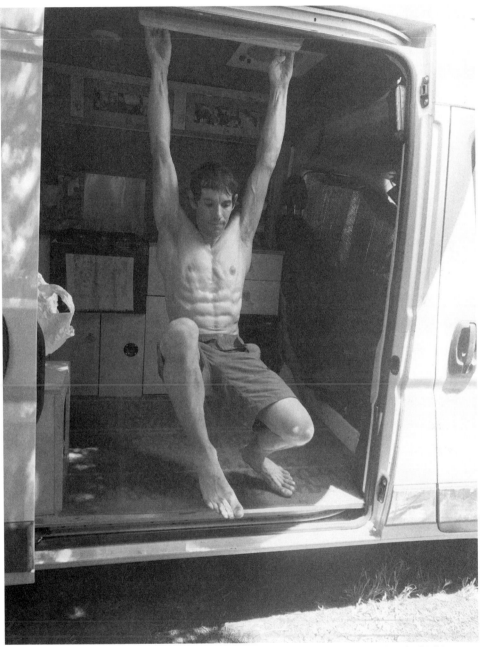

After completion of the climb, Alex told the author that on the way up the wall he was already thinking about his next goal. An hour later, the author took this photo of Alex on his hangboard.

GLOSSARY

ANCHOR: Any device or method for securing a climber to a rock face to prevent a fall, hoist a load, or redirect a rope.

ARETE: An acute edge formed by two intersecting planes of rock. Can be blunt and rounded or sharply defined. The outside corner of a brick building is a good example of an arete.

BELAY: 1. The technique used to hold a rope in order to arrest a falling climber. 2. An anchor, as in, "I'll set up a belay here."

BELAY LOOP: A sewn loop on the front of a harness that a belay device is clipped to for belaying or rappelling.

BELAY/RAPPEL DEVICE: The device through which the rope is passed and clipped to the harness with a locking carabiner. Creates manageable rope friction to both belay a climber and rappel.

BETA: Tips on how to do a climbing sequence, as in, "There's a jug off to the left above the third bolt." Usually told to you by someone who has done the route or problem.

BIVOUAC (or BIVY): 1. (noun) A place to spend the night. 2. (verb) To spend the night, often in an unexpected location.

BOLT: Permanent protection drilled into the rock. Most commonly used as sport-climbing protection and for belay and rappel anchors.

CAM: A spring-loaded protection device. When a trigger is pulled, the cams retract and can be inserted into cracks. When the trigger is released, the cams expand and lock into the crack. When properly placed in solid rock, a cam offers easily removable and bomber protection.

CARABINER (or BINER): An aluminum snap link used for myriad tasks, the primary one being to connect the rope to the anchor.

CHALK: Magnesium carbonate powder applied to hands to keep them dry and improve grip.

CHIMNEY: A crack wide enough for a body to fit inside.

CRIMPER: A small edge just wide enough for fingertips. One "crimps" on a crimper.

CRUX: The hardest section of a climb.

DYNO: A "dynamic" move, often a jump, that allows a climber to gain a distant hold.

FACE CLIMBING: Climbing using features such as knobs, edges, slopers, and tufas. Different from crack climbing, during which you insert your hands and feet into a crack.

FINGER CRACK: A fissure the size of a person's fingers, as deep as fingertips to knuckles.

FINGERLOCK: Camming fingers into cracks. There are a variety of fingerlocks used for different crack sizes.

FIST JAM: A technique used to climb wider cracks by clenching a hand into a fist and inserting it into the slot.

HAND CRACK: A crack wide enough to accept an entire hand, but not so wide that it requires a fist jam.

HAND JAM: A technique used to climb hand cracks by slotting/camming a cupped hand into a crack.

JUG: A large hold. Also referred to as a "bucket."

LEADER: The climber who goes up first, clipping their side of the rope through protection using carabiners or quickdraws.

OFF-WIDTH: A crack too wide for fist jams and too narrow to be a chimney.

ON-SIGHT: Climbing a route without falling or resting on gear and with no prior beta or knowledge of the moves.

PITCH: The distance climbed to reach an anchor point or belay stance. Multi-pitch climbs are found on cliffs taller than one rope length. A single-pitch route requires only one rope length.

PITON: An iron spike (aka "pin") available in various sizes and shapes that can be hammered into and out of cracks and clipped for protection. Pitons scar the rock, and they are typically only used in remote mountain ranges these days.

PROTECTION (or PRO): Equipment placed in the rock to catch a climber's fall.

QUICKDRAW: A short sling with carabiners on each end used to connect the rope to protection, such as bolts and cams.

RACK: A generic term for the collection of gear taken up on a climb. Usually composed of slings, protection, quickdraws, carabiners, and other equipment for getting up and back down.

SEND: Climbing a route without falling or resting on gear. Past tense: sent, e.g., "I sent Freerider."

SMEAR: Friction-dependent foothold, where the ball of the foot is "pasted" over a textured or lower-angled surface in order to gain purchase.

STEM: A technique for climbing corners by holding oneself in place by pushing in opposite directions with the feet and hands.

TOP ROPE: A rope from above that provides security for a climber. A slingshot top rope is a rope that runs from a climber through overhead anchors and back down to a belayer positioned on the ground.

SOURCES

Rockandice.com/how-to-climb/climbing-terminology
Rockclimbing.com

PHOTO CREDITS

pp. ii–iii: © Christian George; pp. 4, 25, 73, 83, 87, 114, 117, 207: © Mark Synnott Collection; p. 13: © Getty Images; p.19: Courtesy of the Frost Family Collection; p. 23: © Peter Doucette; p. 34: © Dierdre Wolownick; p. 39: © Phil Bard; pp. 47, 70: © Dean Fidelman; p. 55: © Celin Serbo; p. 106: © Jane Joseph; p. 197: © Tom Evans; p. 200: © Austin Siadak.

ACKNOWLEDGMENTS

Out of all the people who helped bring these chapters to fruition, no one had a bigger impact than my friend and fellow Crazy Kid Jeff Chapman. If you enjoyed this story, please tip your hat to Jeff, because it's in large part due to the many hours he spent editing, analyzing, and providing feedback on the manuscript.

I am also extremely grateful to *National Geographic* magazine and my editor, Peter Gwin, for assigning me to report on Alex Honnold's historic free solo of El Capitan. Without National Geographic's support and belief in the importance of this story, the book that you are holding would not exist.

Of course, there would be no story to tell without Alex Honnold, to whom I owe an immense debt of gratitude. Thank you, Alex, for being who you are, for your inspiration and support, and for trusting me to get this right. I owe the same thanks to Alex's now wife, Cassandra "Sanni" McCandless, who openly shared her story with me, climbed with me, and even babysat for my son Tommy. I'd also like to thank Alex's mom, Dierdre Honnold Wowolnick, for sharing her many stories about Alex as a youth.

It was serendipitous that around the same time I was developing the proposal for this book, I happened to sit on a panel alongside author Virginia Morell. A huge thanks to Virginia for introducing me to her literary agent, Gillian MacKenzie. Gillian turned out to be not only a kindred spirit, but a brilliant agent. Thanks also to Gillian's business partner, Kirsten Wolf.

We got lucky when Gillian shared *The Impossible Climb* with Aneeka Kalia at Viking, who immediately saw the potential for this book to be adapted for young readers. A huge thanks to Aneeka for her outstanding vision and for guiding us through this process. Additional thanks go to the talented crew at Viking who helped bring this project to fruition, including Jim Hoover, Lucia Baez, Krista Ahlberg, Abigail Powers, Marinda Valenti, Madeline Newquist, Kate Frentzel, Delia Davis, Kaitlin Kneafsey, and last but not least, Viking's publisher, Ken Wright.

I am indebted to Tommy Caldwell, Peter Croft, John Long, Dean Fidelman, Mandi Finger, Ben Smalley, Chris Weidner, Maury Birdwell, Ted Hesser, Colin Haley, Emily Harrington, Brad Gobright, Peter Mortimer, Jim Hurst, Mikey Schaefer, Pablo Durana, Matt Irving, Dave Allfrey, Cheyne Lempe, Joseph LeDoux, Jane Joseph, Henry Barber, Forest Altherr, and Jeff Ball, all of whom generously gave of their time to help me better understand Alex Honnold and some of the other people in this book.

Thank you to Peter Bohler for the cover photo, and to all the other photographers who contributed visuals to this book: Dean Fidelman, Tom Evans, Rob Frost, Peter Doucette, Phil Bard, Christian George, Austin Siadak, and Celin Serbo.

I'd also like to thank all the members of the climbing community, especially those with whom I have roped up over the years: Jimmy Chin, Greg Child, Jeff Achey, Shaun Pinkham, John Climaco, Simon Ahlgren, Christian George, Warren Hollinger, Jerry Gore, Ben Spiess, Rob Frost, Pete Masterson, Jimmy Surette, Scott Lee, Frank Carus, Tom Burt, Jeff Achey, John Climaco, John Catto, Kit Deslauriers, Renan Ozturk, Hazel Findlay, James Pearson, Pete Athans, Jim Zellers, Kasha Rigby, Hilaree Nelson O'Neill, Heidi Wirtz, Cameron Lawson, Mike Pennings, Jeff Hollenbaugh, Ted Hesser, and Bob Snover.

A few climbers in particular deserve special mention: Jared Ogden and Kevin Thaw, with whom I did the bulk of my expeditions; Greg Child, a hero from my Crazy Kids days, who later became a mentor, partner, and friend; and Conrad Anker, for opening the door for me to pursue climbing full time, for mentorship, and for suggesting that I bring Alex Honnold on that expedition to Borneo.

My career as a climber would have followed a very different trajectory were it not for the support and encouragement I've received from the North Face for the past twenty-five years. There are too many of you to mention, but a few of you are: Katie Ramage, Chris Sylvia, Maeve Sloane, Ann Krcik, Kevin Hogan, Andy Coutant, Landon Bassett, James Kelly, Jamie Starr, Matt Sharkey, Todd Spaletto, Steve Rendle, and the entire athlete team.

Thanks to my sister, Amy Synnott-D'Annibale, who set me on the path to becoming a writer when she helped me land my first official magazine assignment back in 1996. She has always been there with sage advice when I needed it. My mom, Suzanne Synnott, instilled in me at a young age that I was special and meant to do great things. My late father, William Synnott, gave me my drive, work ethic, and love for the outdoors. He would have done his best to hide it, but I know he would have been proud to hold this book in his hands.

Thanks to all the writers whose work has been helpful to me in telling this story: David Roberts, John Long, Andrew Bisharat, Alex Lowther, Dougald MacDonald, JB MacKinnon, Joseph Hooper, Daniel Duane, Tommy Caldwell, Benjamin Madley, James Lucas, Seth Heller, Cedar Wright, and Burr Snider.

There's a saying amongst climbers that we are "living the dream." It's almost always said sarcastically, in acknowledgment of the fact that the climbing life is a tricky one, especially when we're not on the wall. No one understands this better than my family. Finding the right balance between my passion for climbing and the responsibilities of being a husband and father has been the greatest challenge of my life. And I'll readily admit that I haven't always gotten it right. But I hope this book might one day help my children—Will, Matt, Lilla, and Tommy—appreciate why this sport is so important to me.

Lastly, I want to thank Hampton, who is by far my biggest supporter and without whom the young reader version of *The Impossible Climb* would not exist. Her contribution as an editor, confidant, mom, athlete, adventurer, best friend, and moral rock cannot be overstated. Thank you, Hampton. I could not have a better partner for the climb through life.